Spelling

ISBN-13: 978-1-4190-3407-7

©2008 Harcourt Achieve Inc.

Steck-Vaughn is a trademark of Harcourt Achieve Inc.

The paper used in this book comes from sustainable resources.

Printed in the United States of America.
6 7 8 9   1413   14 13 12
4500341904

Steck Vaughn™

A Harcourt Achieve Imprint

www.HarcourtSchoolSupply.com
1-800-531-5015

Contents

Introduction

Core Skills: Spelling is a research-based, systematic spelling program developed to help students master spelling. The program is based on three critical goals for students:

- to learn to spell common spelling patterns and troublesome words
- to learn strategies related to sounds and spelling patterns
- to link spelling and meaning

Each book in the *Core Skills: Spelling* program is composed of 30 skill lessons. The majority of skill lessons in this program focus on spellings of vowel sounds. Other skill lessons focus on word structure and content-area words.

Key features of this book include:

- study steps that focus learning,

- a spelling table that contains common spellings for consonant and vowel sounds,

- lessons that build competency and provide visual reinforcement,

- word study that expands vocabulary and meaning,

- engaging vocabulary and context activities that encourage students to explore word meanings and use words in meaningful contexts, and

- challenge sections that present opportunities to enrich vocabulary and extend spelling skills.

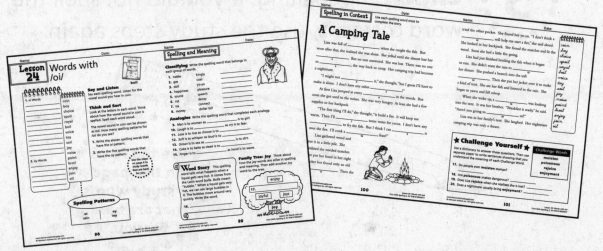

Study Steps to Learn a Word

 Say the word. What consonant sounds do you hear? What vowel sounds do you hear? How many syllables do you hear?

 Look at the letters in the word. Think about how each sound is spelled. Find any spelling patterns or parts that you know. Close your eyes. Picture the word in your mind.

 Spell the word aloud.

 Write the word. Say each letter as you write it.

 Check the spelling. If you did not spell the word correctly, use the study steps again.

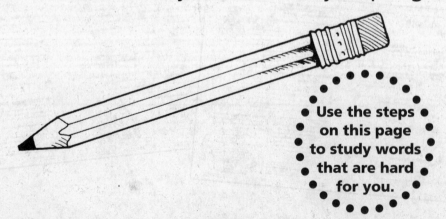

Use the steps on this page to study words that are hard for you.

Spelling Table

Sound	Spellings	Examples	Sound	Spellings	Examples
/ă/	a a_e ai au	ask, have, plaid, laugh	/ŏ/	o a	shop, was
/ā/	a a_e ai ay ea eigh ey	table, save, rain, gray, break, eight, they	/ō/	o o_e oa oe ou ow	both, hole, road, toe, boulder, slow
/ä/	a ea	father, heart	/oi/	oi oy	point, enjoy
/âr/	air are ere	chair, care, where	/ô/	o oa oo ou ough a au aw	off, coarse, door, four, brought, tall, autumn, draw
/b/	b bb	best, rabbit			
/ch/	ch tch	child, catch	/o͝o/	oo ou u u_e	book, could, pull, sure
/d/	d dd	dish, add			
/ĕ/	e ea ie ue a ai ay	best, read, friend, guess, many, said, says	/o͞o/	oo ou u_e ue ew o	noon, you, June, blue, news, two
/ē/	e e_e ea ee ei eo ey y	even, these, each, meet, receive, people, key, city	/ou/	ou ow	about, owl
			/p/	p pp	place, dropped
/f/	f ff gh	fly, off, laugh	/r/	r rr wr	rain, sorry, write
/g/	g gg	go, egg	/s/	s ss c	safe, dress, city
/h/	h wh	hot, who	/sh/	sh s	shook, sure
/ĭ/	i ui e ee u a	inside, build, pretty, been, busy, luggage	/t/	t tt ed	take, matter, thanked
/ī/	i i_e ie igh eye uy y	tiny, drive, pie, high, eyes, buy, fly	/th/	th	then
			/th/	th	third
/îr/	ear eer eir ere	year, deer, weird, here	/ŭ/	u o oe	such, mother, does
/j/	j g	jog, danger	/ûr/	ur ir er or ear ere our	curl, girl, dessert, world, learn, were, flourish
/k/	k c ck ch	keep, coat, kick, school			
/ks/	x	six	/v/	v f	even, of
/kw/	qu	quiet	/w/	w wh o	walk, when, one
/l/	l ll	late, tell	/y/	y	year
/m/	m mb mm	much, comb, hammer	/yo͞o/	u_e ew ue	use, few, Tuesday
/n/	n kn nn	need, know, beginning	/z/	z zz s	sneeze, blizzard, says
/ng/	n ng	thank, bring	/ə/	a e i o u	along, misery, estimate, lion, subtract

Core Skills Spelling 3, SV 9781419034077

Lesson 1
Words with Short *a*

catch

1. *a* Words

Short
Short
Short
Short
Short
Short
Short
Long

laugh
loung
Lang
Lung
Lung
Laung

2. *au* Word

y

ask
matter
black
add
match
Saturday
class
apple
subtract
laugh
thank
catch
January
after
hammer
half

Say and Listen
Say each spelling word. Listen for the short *a* sound.

Think and Sort
Look at the letters in each word. Think about how short *a* is spelled. Spell each word aloud.

Short a can be shown as /ă/. How many spelling patterns for /ă/ do you see?

1. Write the spelling words that have the *a* pattern.

2. Write the spelling word that has the *au* pattern.

Use the steps on page 4 to study words that are hard for you.

Spelling Patterns

a	**au**
m**a**tch	l**au**gh

Name: _____   Date: _____

Spelling and Meaning

Definitions Write the spelling word for each definition.
Use a dictionary if you need to.

1. to find the sum   _____
2. problem   _____
3. to look alike   _____
4. group of students   _____
5. following   _____
6. to say one is grateful   _____
7. one of two equal parts   _____
8. to request   _____

Classifying Write the spelling word that belongs in each group.

9. banana   orange   pear   _____
10. add   multiply   divide   _____
11. screwdriver saw   drill   _____
12. white   green   yellow   _____
13. chuckle   grin   smile   _____
14. March   April   September   _____
15. run   throw   pitch   _____

Word Story   One of the spelling words comes from two Old English words. The first is *Saeter*. The second is *daeg*. *Saeter* was the name for the Roman god Saturn. *Daeg* meant "day." Write the word.

16. _____

Family Tree: *thank* Think about how the *thank* words are alike in spelling and meaning. Then add another *thank* word to the tree.

thanks

17. _____

thanking   thankless

thank

Lesson 1: Words with Short *a*
Core Skills Spelling 3, SV 9781419034077

Spelling in Context

Use each spelling word once to complete the selection.

Cold Relief

Your head feels as if it is being pounded with a _____.
                                                        1
Your eyes are so itchy and watery that you can't see well. You put on socks

that do not _____. Your throat hurts. You sniffle and sneeze
             2
your way through every _____ at school. What is the
                        3
_____? You have a cold!
 4

You may think that you _____ colds from cold, wet weather.
                        5
This is not true. Icy winds in _____ or February do not cause
                                6
colds. You can _____ tiny germs called cold viruses for your
                7
sniffles and sneezes.

Cold germs travel in the air
and on people's hands, so you
should wash your hands often.
Washing your hands is especially
important _____
            8
being around someone else
who has a cold. You can also
_____ people who
 9
sneeze to cover their mouth.

There is no cure for the
common cold, but there are some
things you can do to make you feel better. Drink at least _____ a
                                                                      10

glass of fruit juice or water every hour. A full glass is even better.

     People say that an _____ a day keeps
11

the doctor away. It is true that apples and other good foods help make your body strong. When you have a cold, _____ extra fruits and vegetables to your meals.
12

At the same time, _____ junk food.
13

     Some people think that chicken soup is the best medicine for a cold. Do not _____. Hot soup really can
14

make you feel better. Some people say that adding a little bit of _____ pepper makes the soup work even better.
15

     When you have a cold, stay in bed and rest. This is true even if it is a sunny _____ morning. If you take
16

good care of yourself, you should feel better in no time!

ask
matter
black
add
match
Saturday
class
apple
subtract
laugh
thank
catch
January
after
hammer
half

★ Challenge Yourself ★

Challenge Words

plaid   **agony**
clank   **fragile**

Use a dictionary to answer these questions. Then use separate paper to write sentences showing that you understand the meaning of each Challenge Word.

17. Does a **plaid** shirt have one color or many colors? _____

18. Would you be in **agony** if you hit your thumb with a hammer? _____

19. Could an old iron gate **clank** when you shut it? _____

20. Would it be safe to play in a **fragile** tree house? _____

Name: _____   Date: _____

Lesson 2

Words with Long *a*

break

1. *a*-consonant-*e* Words

_____
_____
_____
_____
_____
_____
_____
_____
_____

2. *ay* Words

_____
_____
_____
_____

3. *ea* Words

_____
_____

4. *a* Word

_____

gray
page
great
change
April
face
save
away
break
ate
place
pay
late
safe
May
came

Say and Listen

Say each spelling word. Listen for the long *a* sound.

Think and Sort

Look at the letters in each word. Think about how long *a* is spelled. Spell each word aloud.

Long *a* can be shown as /ā/. How many spelling patterns for /ā/ do you see?

1. Write the nine spelling words that have the *a*-consonant-*e* pattern.

2. Write the four spelling words that have the *ay* pattern.

3. Write the two spelling words that have the *ea* pattern.

4. Write the one spelling word that has the *a* pattern.

Use the steps on page 4 to study words that are hard for you.

Spelling Patterns

a-consonant-e	ay	ea	a
f**a**c**e**	M**ay**	br**ea**k	**A**pril

Lesson 2: Words with Long a
Core Skills Spelling 3, SV 9781419034077

Spelling and Meaning

Synonyms Synonyms are words that have the same meaning. Write the spelling word that is a synonym for each word below.

1. arrived _____
2. unhurt _____
3. absent _____
4. put _____
5. messenger _____
6. wonderful _____
7. switch _____
8. silvery _____

Anagrams An anagram is a word whose letters can be used to make another word. Write the spelling word that contains the letters of the underlined anagram in each sentence.

9. Jenna's birthday is in the month of <u>yaM</u>. _____
10. The team <u>tea</u> pizza after the game. _____
11. Please do not <u>brake</u> my pencil. _____
12. Ten dollars is too much to <u>yap</u>. _____
13. The bus was <u>tale</u> this morning. _____
14. Let's <u>vase</u> the best for last. _____
15. The baby had a big smile on her <u>cafe</u>. _____

Word Story Many English words come from other languages. One spelling word comes from the Latin word *Aprilis*. *Aprilis* was the name of the second month in the Roman calendar. It names one of the spring months. Write the spelling word.

16. _____

Family Tree: *pay* Think about how the *pay* words are alike in spelling and meaning. Then add another *pay* word to the tree.

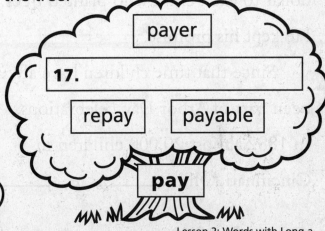

payer

17. _____

repay   payable

pay

Spelling in Context

Use each spelling word once to complete the selection.

A Special Day

Arbor Day is a special holiday. The word *arbor* means "tree." Arbor Day

helps people remember to plant new trees and to _____ older

     1

ones. It can help _____ people's ideas about Earth and the

     2

environment.

Arbor Day was started by a Nebraska man named Sterling Morton in 1872.

Mr. Morton loved trees. He asked everyone in the state to plant trees on a

day he called Arbor Day. He wanted to give prizes to those who planted the

most trees. A million trees were planted. Imagine the look on Mr. Morton's

_____! He was very surprised and pleased. The day was a

     3

_____ success.

     4

Soon people in other states started to celebrate Arbor Day, too.

In 1876 a man in Connecticut wanted to honor the nation's

hundredth birthday. The man invited

children to plant trees. He said he

would _____ one

     5

dollar to each child who planted trees.

He kept his promise.

Since that time children have always

been part of Arbor Day celebrations.

In 1882 almost 20,000 children in

Cincinnati, Ohio, _____

     6

from many schools to the city's Eden Park. They planted new
trees. They were careful not to _____ any leaves
  7
or branches. Then the children named each tree after a famous
person. Perhaps they _____ a picnic lunch.
                       8
They might even have read a _____ from a
                             9
book about _____ squirrels.
              10

   Over the years Arbor Day celebrations have taken
_____ in city parks, public squares, and
    11
schools. Today both children and adults take part in Arbor
Day events. Many people celebrate Arbor Day in March,
_____, or _____. Others
    12   13
celebrate in _____ fall or winter. Japan, China,
              14
and other countries far _____ celebrate this
                          15
holiday, too. Arbor Day is an important day. It is a day to think
about trees and ways to help keep them _____.
                                         16
This special day gives people a time to plant new life.

- gray
- page
- great
- change
- April
- face
- save
- away
- break
- ate
- place
- pay
- late
- safe
- May
- came

★ Challenge Yourself ★

Challenge Words

cable	debate
dismay	labor

What do you think each Challenge Word means?
Check a dictionary to see if you are right. Then use
separate paper to write sentences showing that you
understand the meaning of each Challenge Word.

17. A **cable** holds up the bridge.
18. She will **debate** whether to buy a new bike or fix her old one.
19. I watched in **dismay** as my hat fell in the mud.
20. Riding up the steep hill required a great deal of **labor.**

Lesson 3

More Words with Long *a*

train

1. *ai* Words
_____
_____
_____
_____
_____
_____

2. *a* Words
_____
_____
_____
_____
_____

3. *eigh* Words
_____
_____

4. *ey* Word
_____

fable
rain
danger
sail
afraid
table
aid
train
eight
wait
able
aim
weigh
they
paint
paper

Say and Listen
Say each spelling word. Listen for the long *a* sound.

Think and Sort
Look at the letters in each word. Think about how long *a* is spelled. Spell each word aloud.

Long *a* can be shown as /ā/. How many spelling patterns for /ā/ do you see?

1. Write the eight spelling words that have the *ai* pattern.

2. Write the five spelling words that have the *a* pattern.

3. Look at the word *eight*. The spelling pattern for this word is *eigh*. The *g* and *h* are silent. Write the two spelling words that have the *eigh* pattern.

4. Write the one spelling word that has the *ey* pattern.

Use the steps on page 4 to study words that are hard for you.

Spelling Patterns

ai	a	eigh	ey
r**ai**n	p**a**per	w**eigh**	th**ey**

Spelling and Meaning

Antonyms Antonyms are words that have opposite meanings.
Write the spelling word that is an antonym of each word below.

1. hurt _____
2. fearless _____
3. go _____
4. safety _____
5. unable _____

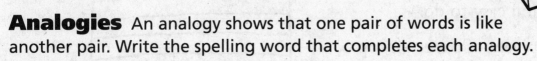

Analogies An analogy shows that one pair of words is like
another pair. Write the spelling word that completes each analogy.

6. *Bedspread* is to *bed* as *tablecloth* is to _____.
7. *Two* is to *four* as *four* is to _____.
8. *Car* is to *road* as _____ is to *track*.
9. *Engine* is to *car* as _____ is to *sailboat*.
10. *Story* is to _____ as *animal* is to *dog*.
11. *Silk* is to *smooth* as _____ is to *wet*.
12. *We* is to *us* as _____ is to *them*.
13. *Oven* is to *bake* as *scale* is to _____.
14. *Ink* is to *pen* as _____ is to *brush*.
15. *Easy* is to *simple* as _____ is to *point*.

Word Story   Long ago
some people wrote on papyrus.
Papyrus was made of dried grass.
Today most people use another
material to write on. It is made
of finely cut wood. The name of
this material comes from the word
papyrus. Write the word.

16. _____

Family Tree: *paint* Think about
how the *paint* words are alike in spelling
and meaning. Then add another *paint*
word to the tree.

paints

17. _____

painter   repaint

paint

Spelling in Context

Use each spelling word once to complete the selection.

Make Your Own Village

What can you do when you can't go outside and play because of _____ 1? Make your own village! It's fun and easy to do.

First spread pieces of paper on top of a _____ 2. Then cut more pieces of _____ 3 into strips. Mix one cup of flour with enough water to make a thin paste. Gather seven or _____ 4 small boxes to use for buildings.

Next get a towel and wet it. Keep it near you as you work. The wet towel will _____ 5 you in cleaning your sticky hands.

Dip the strips of paper into the paste. Don't be _____ 6 to use a lot of paste. Wind the paper strips around the boxes. You will be _____ 7 to make buildings of different shapes by using more strips in some places.

You should _____ 8 to work until you have covered all your buildings with paper strips. Then let the buildings dry. You will probably have to _____ 9 a day or two.

Later get some _____ 10 and brushes and paint your buildings. Then you are ready to make the ground. Spread the paste over wrinkled paper.

Paint your ground green after the paste dries and then paint a

lake. Make a boat to _____ on the lake.
                            11

Do you think your village needs a _____?
                                              12
You can make one by using old matchboxes for the cars. Make

the train tracks out of toothpicks. For train wheels, buttons

work well because _____ are small and round.
                        13

You can also add mountains and bridges to your village.

You can even add a sign that says "Falling Rock" to warn of

_____.
      14

What is missing from your village? People! Make clay

people. If they don't _____ too much, you can
                              15
sit them in your boat without making it turn over. You can

also use the people to act out a _____ or other
                                        16
kind of story. Have fun playing with your village!

Word List

- fable
- rain
- danger
- sail
- afraid
- table
- aid
- train
- eight
- wait
- able
- aim
- weigh
- they
- paint
- paper

★ Challenge Yourself ★

Challenge Words

frail	agent
maintain	contain

Use a dictionary to answer these questions. Then use separate paper to write sentences showing that you understand the meaning of each Challenge Word.

17. Would a bridge made of toothpicks be **frail**? _____

18. Could a secret **agent** work for a government? _____

19. Is it important to **maintain** a town's bridges and roads? _____

20. Are jars that **contain** jam empty? _____

Lesson 4

Words with Short *e*

egg

1. *e* Words

_____
_____
_____
_____
_____
_____
_____
_____
_____
_____

2. *ea* Words

_____
_____
_____

3. *ai* Words

_____
_____

4. *ay* Word

_____

next
egg
says
ready
end
help
spent
again
second
forget
dress
said
address
read
test
head

Say and Listen

Say each spelling word. Listen for the short e sound.

Think and Sort

Look at the letters in each word. Think about how short e is spelled. Spell each word aloud.

Short e can be shown as /ĕ/. How many spelling patterns for /ĕ/ do you see?

1. Write the ten spelling words that have the e pattern.

2. Write the three spelling words that have the ea pattern.

3. Write the two spelling words that have the *ai* pattern.

4. Write the one spelling word that has the *ay* pattern.

Use the steps on page 4 to study words that are hard for you.

Spelling Patterns

e	ea	ai	ay
dr**e**ss	h**ea**d	s**ai**d	s**ay**s

Name: _____ Date: _____

Spelling and Meaning

Clues Write the spelling word for each clue.

1. includes a ZIP code   _____
2. once more   _____
3. what is done to a book   _____
4. opposite of *remember*   _____
5. used your money   _____
6. all set   _____
7. aid   _____
8. I say, you say, he _____ _____

Classifying Write the spelling word that belongs in each group.

9. hour   minute   _____
10. exam   quiz   _____
11. spoke   told   _____
12. first   then   _____
13. stop   quit   _____
14. blouse   skirt   _____
15. toast   juice   _____

Word Story The phrase "raining cats and dogs" is called an **idiom**. In an idiom, the meanings of the words don't add up to the meaning of the phrase. Write the spelling word that completes each idiom below.

He **kept his** ____ when he got lost.
Don't **lose your** ____ during a storm.

16. _____

Family Tree: *help* Think about how the *help* words are alike in spelling and meaning. Then add another *help* word to the tree.

helping

17. _____

helps   helpful

help

Core Skills Spelling 3, SV 9781419034077

Spelling in Context

Use each spelling word once to complete the story.

ME-2

ME-2 was a little robot with a big problem. She had a very bad memory. On Friday morning ME-2 ate bread and a scrambled _____.

 1

Then she forgot that she had eaten breakfast, so she ate it _____.

 2

On Saturday morning she put on blue jeans. Then she forgot what she had planned to wear, so she put on her best _____, too.

 3

Things were bad at home. They were no better at school. When her teacher asked her a question about a story, ME-2 forgot what she had

_____. When the teacher gave the class a _____,

 4   **5**

ME-2 had forgotten to study for it. She was never _____ for

 6

gym because she always forgot her sneakers.

One day ME-2 forgot where she lived. She had forgotten her

own _____! ME-2

 7

_____ the night with her

 8

best friend, US-2.

ME-2's mother was very worried. She found ME-2 at school early the very

_____ day. ME-2's mother

 9

_____, "This won't happen

 10

a _____ time. You are going

 11

to the doctor."

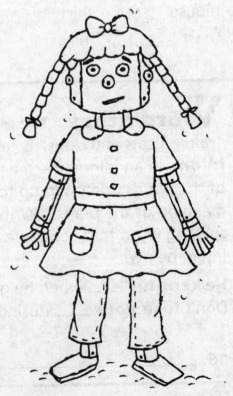

www.harcourtschoolsupply.com
20
Lesson 4: Words with Short e
Core Skills Spelling 3, SV 9781419034077

The doctor gave ME-2 a checkup. Soon it was over. ME-2 told her mother, "The doctor _____ I'm
__12__
just fine. I wish I could remember why you brought me here."

"Doctor, how can ME-2 be fine?" asked her mother. "She would lose her _____ if it was not screwed on
__13__
her shoulders! Can't you _____ her?"
__14__

The mother's words gave the doctor an idea. He looked at the screws in ME-2's head. Sure enough, one screw was loose. He fixed it. That put an _____ to ME-2's bad
__15__
memory.

"Oh, no! I just remembered something," cried ME-2. "We get report cards tomorrow. That is something I wish I could
_____!"
__16__

next
egg
says
ready
end
help
spent
again
second
forget
dress
said
address
read
test
head

★ Challenge Yourself ★

Challenge Words

**genuine
athletic
attempt
celebration**

What do you think each Challenge Word means? Check a dictionary to see if you are right. Then use separate paper to write sentences showing that you understand the meaning of each Challenge Word.

17. ME-2 was a **genuine** robot.
18. She liked gym class because she was **athletic**.
19. The doctor's first **attempt** to help ME-2 did not work.
20. They had a **celebration** when ME-2 got a good report card.

Name: _____ Date: _____

Lesson 5

Plural Words

apples

1. -s Plurals

_____
_____
_____
_____
_____
_____
_____
_____
_____
_____

2. -es Plurals

_____
_____
_____
_____

tests
pages
papers
dresses
hammers
tables
clowns
classes
paints
apples
eggs
matches
hands
trains
addresses
places

Say and Listen
Say the spelling words. Listen for the ending sounds.

Think and Sort
All of the spelling words are plural words. **Plural** words name more than one thing. Most plural words are formed by adding -s.

boy + **s** = boy**s**   page + **s** = page**s**

Singular words name one thing. If a singular word ends in s, ss, ch, or x, -es is added to form the plural.

glass + **es** = glass**es**

1. Write the twelve spelling words that are formed by adding -s.

2. Write the four spelling words that are formed by adding -es.

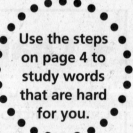

Use the steps on page 4 to study words that are hard for you.

Spelling Patterns

-s	-es
test**s**	dress**es**
page**s**	

Spelling and Meaning

Making Connections Complete each sentence with the spelling word that goes with the workers.

1. Artists use brushes and _____.
2. Carpenters work with nails and _____.
3. Fruit farmers grow oranges and _____.
4. Cooks work with milk and _____.
5. Teachers grade projects and _____.
6. Writers work with _____ in books.
7. Tailors sew skirts and _____.
8. Mail carriers work with names and _____.

Definitions Write the spelling word for each definition. Use a dictionary if you need to.

9. questions that measure knowledge _____
10. small sticks of wood used to light fires _____
11. connected railroad cars _____
12. part of the arms below the wrists _____
13. particular areas _____
14. circus performers who make people laugh _____
15. groups of students taught by the same teacher _____

Word Story   One spelling word comes from the Latin word *tabula*. A *tabula* was a board or plank. The spelling word that comes from *tabula* names things on which we set our food or play games. Write the word.

16. _____

Family Tree: hands *Hands* is a form of *hand*. Think about how the *hand* words are alike in spelling and meaning. Then add another *hand* word to the tree.

handle

17. _____

hands   handful

hand

Spelling in Context

Use each spelling word once to complete the selection.

Behind the Scenes

When many people think of movie artists, they think of actors. Actors are important, but other kinds of movie artists are important, too.

Makeup artists work on the actors. They make the actors look like the characters they are playing. Makeup artists brush face _____

__1__ onto actors to make them look funny, scary, or old. These artists may also use makeup on actors' arms and _____

__2__ so that all of the skin looks the same.

Costume artists plan and help make the clothes actors wear. These include fancy gowns and other kinds of _____ from the past.

__3__

Costume artists also make silly baggy pants for actors who play circus _____. They

__4__ even make animal costumes for actors to wear.

Other movie artists make the movie sets, or the _____ where the stories take place. They use saws,

__5__

wood, _____, and nails to make rooms. They also build

__6__

_____, chairs, and other pieces of furniture for the set.

__7__

Prop artists find the objects actors need. A movie script may say that actors eat fruit in one part of the movie. A prop artist must find shiny red

_____. In another part of the movie, an actor may have to light

__8__

a fire. A prop artist must have wood and _____ on hand.

__9__

Other artists work with special sounds in movies. A movie may call for the sound of _____ frying.
10
A sound artist might crumple _____ to make
11
the sound. The movie might also call for the sound of two

_____ racing down a railroad track. A sound
12
artist might record real trains. A sound artist puts all sounds

through several different _____ to make sure
13
they sound real.

Would you like to be a movie artist? You can
start by working on school plays. You can take special

_____, too. You can also look in the yellow
14

_____ of the telephone book. Find the
15

_____ and telephone numbers of children's
16
theaters near you. Get behind the scenes!

tests
pages
papers
dresses
hammers
tables
clowns
classes
paints
apples
eggs
matches
hands
trains
addresses
places

★ Challenge Yourself ★

Challenge Words

losses	meteors
caverns	neckties

Write the Challenge Word for each clue. Use a dictionary to see if you are right. Then use separate paper to write sentences showing that you understand the meaning of each Challenge Word

17. These look like bright streaks of light in the sky. _____

18. This word is made from two shorter words put together. _____

19. These can make ball players sad. _____

20. You might find bats in these. _____

Lesson 6

More Words with Short *e*

cents

1. *e* Words

_____
_____
_____
_____
_____
_____
_____
_____
_____
_____
_____
_____
_____

2. *ie* Word

_____

3. *a* Word

_____

4. *ue* Word

_____

slept
February
them
never
when
many
sent
kept
September
best
friend
then
cents
Wednesday
guess
better

Say and Listen

Say each spelling word. Listen for the short e sound.

Think and Sort

Look at the letters in each word. Think about how short e is spelled. Spell each word aloud.

Short e can be shown as /ĕ/. How many spelling patterns for /ĕ/ do you see?

1. Write the thirteen spelling words that have the e pattern.

2. Write the one spelling word that has the *ie* pattern.

3. Write the one spelling word that has the *a* pattern.

4. Write the one spelling word that has the *ue* pattern.

Use the steps on page 4 to study words that are hard for you.

Spelling Patterns

e	ie	a	ue
b**e**st	fri**e**nd	m**a**ny	g**ue**ss

Name: _____ Date: _____

Spelling and Meaning

Classifying Write the spelling word that belongs in each group.

1. pal   buddy   _____
2. lots   several   _____
3. July   August   _____
4. Monday   Tuesday   _____
5. rested   napped   _____
6. December January   _____
7. good   better   _____
8. mailed   shipped   _____
9. who   what   _____

Rhymes Write the spelling word that completes each sentence and rhymes with the underlined word.

10. If you don't have a <u>pen</u>, _____ I will lend you one.
11. No one <u>slept</u> because the dog _____ us up.
12. Tell _____ to <u>hem</u> the curtains.
13. Have you ever read a _____ <u>letter</u>?
14. Let me _____ who made this <u>mess</u>.
15. I _____ knew you were so <u>clever</u>.

Word Story The Latin word *centum* meant "hundred." Several English words come from *centum*. A *century* is one hundred years. A *centipede* is an animal with one hundred legs. Write the spelling word that means "hundredths of a dollar."

16. _____

Family Tree: *friend* Think about how the *friend* words are alike in spelling and meaning. Then add another *friend* word to the tree.

friendless

17. _____

friends

friend

Spelling in Context

Use each spelling word once to complete the story.

Lily

It was the month of _____, so it was very cold in

New Jersey. Lan and her family were going to sunny Florida on

_____. Before they left,
2

Lan took her pet frog to Carlos. "I'm

so glad you are going to take care of

Lily for me," she told him. "This frog is

the _____ pet I've ever
3

had. Take her home in this shoebox.

I'll pick her up on Saturday."

"This is great! I like frogs," said

Carlos. He took the shoebox home. But when he opened it, Lily

jumped out. Carlos couldn't find Lily anywhere in the house. "I'll

_____ find Lily," he groaned. "I guess I should have
4

_____ the box closed."
5

Carlos went to bed worried. That night while he _____,
6

he dreamed about Lily. He woke up even more worried. At school that day,

he told his _____ Cody what had happened. "Lan is coming
7

back in two days. I have to find Lily by _____," Carlos said in
8

a shaky voice.

Cody said, "I have a _____ idea. Let's go to the pet store and
9

buy another frog. Lan will never _____ that it's not Lily."
10

The pet store had _____ frogs. Carlos and
Cody looked at _____ all. They found one
that looked just like Lily.

"Five dollars," said the sales clerk.

"We have only sixty _____," said Carlos
sadly. The clerk _____ the boys away.

On Saturday morning Lan came to get Lily. Carlos
opened the door. He didn't know what to say. Suddenly he
heard a croak. Lily jumped out of his jacket pocket.

"Lily!" cried Lan happily. "Thanks for taking such
good care of her, Carlos. Would you take care of her
again _____ we visit my grandmother in
_____?"

Carlos looked at Lily and smiled.

slept
February
them
never
when
many
sent
kept
September
best
friend
then
cents
Wednesday
guess
better

★ Challenge Yourself ★

Challenge Words

sketch
index
blend
friendliness

Write the Challenge Word for each clue. Check a
dictionary to see if you are right. Then use separate
paper to write sentences showing that you
understand the meaning of each Challenge Word.

17. When you do this, you mix things.

_____

18. This makes people feel liked. _____

19. You can use this to find something in a book. _____

20. It helps to do this before you make a final drawing. _____

Lesson 7

Words with Long *e*

read

1. *ee* Words

_____
_____
_____
_____
_____
_____
_____
_____

2. *ea* Words

_____
_____
_____
_____
_____
_____
_____

3. *eo* Word

_____

street
please
free
wheel
read
queen
each
sneeze
people
meet
team
sea
need
dream
sleep
meat

Say and Listen

Say each spelling word. Listen for the long e sound.

Think and Sort

Look at the letters in each word. Think about how long e is spelled. Spell each word aloud.

Long e can be shown as /ē/. How many spelling patterns for /ē/ do you see?

1. Write the eight spelling words that have the ee pattern.

2. Write the seven spelling words that have the ea pattern.

3. Write the one spelling word that has the eo pattern.

Use the steps on page 4 to study words that are hard for you.

Spelling Patterns

ee	ea	eo
m**ee**t	t**ea**m	p**eo**ple

Spelling and Meaning

Analogies Write the spelling word that completes each analogy.

1. *Sit* is to *chair* as _____ is to *bed*.
2. *Train* is to *track* as *car* is to _____.
3. *Hives* are to *bees* as *houses* are to _____.
4. *Cough* is to *mouth* as _____ is to *nose*.
5. *Book* is to _____ as *movie* is to *watch*.
6. *Rectangle* is to *door* as *circle* is to _____.
7. *Bush* is to *shrub* as *ocean* is to _____.

Definitions Write the spelling word for each definition.
Use a dictionary if you need to.

8. food from the flesh of animals _____
9. a group of people playing on the same side _____
10. to think, feel, or see during sleep _____
11. to come together _____
12. without cost _____
13. to give pleasure or happiness to _____
14. every one _____
15. must have _____

Word Story The Old Saxon word *quan* meant "wife." Later it became the Old English word *cwen*, which meant "wife, woman, or wife of the king." What do we say today instead of *cwen*? Write the spelling word.

16. _____

Family Tree: *read* Think about how the *read* words are alike in spelling and meaning. Then add another *read* word to the tree.

reread

17.

reads   readable

read

Name: _____   Date: _____

Spelling in Context

Use each spelling word once to complete the story.

Queen of the Roads

Many years ago in a castle by the

_____, there lived a wonderful
            1

_____. All of the _____
            2   3

in her kingdom loved her. But the queen was

not happy. No one at the castle would let her

do any work. Every morning she had to sit and

_____ a book. Every afternoon she
            4

had to _____ the kings and queens
                    5

who came to visit. She even had to eat roasted

_____ for every meal.
            6

When she went to _____ at night,
                                7

the queen would often _____ of a different life. One morning
                                  8

she woke up early. She told a servant, "I _____ to get away from
                                                        9

the castle. I want some time to think. _____ get a carriage ready."
                                                      10

The servant did as he was asked. In no time at all, the queen was driving

down the main _____ of the city. "How can I be useful?" she
                          11

asked herself.

The queen traveled far away. The road became bumpy and dusty. She

was thinking about being a farmer when her carriage hit a hole in the road. A

_____ flew off and got stuck between two large rocks. The
            12

queen tried and tried but couldn't get the wheel _____.
                                                                          13

It was getting dark and cold. She began to shake and

_____.
14

At last two farmers came by. "Thank goodness you are
here!" said the queen. "Will you help me?"

"Of course!" said the farmers. They helped the queen free
the wheel and put it back on the carriage.

"We are a great _____!" said the happy
15

queen. She felt special inside. "How can I thank you?"

"We need new roads that are easy for everyone to travel
on," said the farmers.

"New roads you shall have," answered the queen. "And I
shall help build _____ and every one!"
16

The queen made many new friends. She stayed busy
building new roads with others. After a while everyone began
to call her Queen of the Roads. She was never unhappy again.

Word List
street
please
free
wheel
read
queen
each
sneeze
people
meet
team
sea
need
dream
sleep
meat

★ Challenge Yourself ★

Challenge Words

deceive
feat
seam
teenager

What do you think each Challenge Word means?
Check a dictionary to see if you are right. Then use
separate paper to write sentences showing that you
understand the meaning of each Challenge Word.

17. An honest queen does not **deceive** the people
in her kingdom.
18. The young knight performed a brave **feat**.
19. I ripped the **seam** in my jacket.
20. I will be a **teenager** when I am thirteen.

Lesson 8
More Words with Long e

family

Say and Listen
Say each spelling word. Listen for the long e sound.

Think and Sort
Look at the letters in each word. Think about how long e is spelled. Spell each word aloud.

Long e can be shown as /ē/. How many spelling patterns for /ē/ do you see?

1. Write the one spelling word that has the e pattern.

2. Write the thirteen spelling words that have the y pattern.

3. Write the one spelling word that has the e-consonant-e pattern.

4. Write the one spelling word that has the ey pattern.

Use the steps on page 4 to study words that are hard for you.

1. e Word
_____

2. y Words
_____
_____
_____
_____
_____
_____
_____
_____
_____
_____
_____
_____

3. e-consonant-e Word
_____

4. ey Word
_____

only
story
key
family
sleepy
carry
sunny
these
funny
very
every
city
penny
even
happy
busy

Spelling Patterns

e	y	e-consonant-e	ey
even	stor**y**	th**ese**	k**ey**

Spelling and Meaning

Definitions Write the spelling word for each definition.
Use a dictionary if you need to.

1. to take from one place to another _____
2. extremely _____
3. the most important part _____
4. laughable _____
5. each _____
6. one cent _____
7. nearby items _____
8. a telling of something that happened _____
9. just _____

Antonyms Write the spelling word that is an antonym of the underlined word.

10. Seth was <u>sad</u> when summer camp began. _____
11. We will go to the zoo on a <u>cloudy</u> day. _____
12. Saturday was a <u>lazy</u> day for everyone. _____
13. Life in the <u>country</u> can be very exciting. _____
14. Kara felt <u>lively</u> after reading a book. _____
15. Twelve is an <u>odd</u> number. _____

Word Story Long ago in Rome, rich people had servants. The servants were called *familia*. As time passed, a husband, wife, their children, and their servants were called a *familia*. What spelling word comes from *familia*? Write the word.

16. _____

Family Tree: *happy* Think about how the *happy* words are alike in spelling and meaning. Then add another *happy* word to the tree.

happiest

17. _____

happier   unhappiest

happy

Spelling in Context

Use each spelling word once to complete the selection.

The Best Job in the World

Do you like to draw? Jerry Pinkney loved to draw when he was a child. Today he draws pictures for children's books.

Jerry Pinkney was born in 1939. He grew up in the _____
1
of Philadelphia, Pennsylvania. There were six children in his

_____. The Pinkneys were not rich. They had to watch every
2

_____.
3

Jerry was a pleasant and _____ child. He spent a lot of
4
time with his family. One year an aunt and uncle bought a farm. During the summer the whole family gathered there on weekends. Jerry and his cousins helped the grownups build a house. They had outdoor cookouts on warm, _____ days. When the children grew tired and
5
_____ at night, they slept under the stars.
6

Young Jerry liked to draw _____ much. An artist
7
friend, John Liney, wanted to help him. Liney gave Jerry art supplies, which Jerry would _____ home. Even though Jerry was
8
_____ 11 years old, he knew he wanted to be an artist.
9

In high school Jerry took _____ art class the school offered.
10
He _____ went to night school. After high school Jerry studied
11
art in college for more than two years.

After college Jerry worked as a truck driver and a designer in a flower shop. He knew that _____ **12** jobs were not right for him. He kept drawing and never gave up his dream. Never giving up may have been the _____ to his later success. **13**

Soon Jerry got a job designing greeting cards. Then he got the chance to draw pictures for a book. The book was a _____ that retold an African folk tale. Jerry has **14** been _____ drawing for stories and books ever **15** since.

Today Jerry Pinkney is a famous artist. He has drawn pictures for many books. Some are serious books, but others are _____ books. Pinkney also shares his talent **16** by teaching young people to draw. Some people think he has the best job in the world.

only
story
key
family
sleepy
carry
sunny
these
funny
very
every
city
penny
even
happy
busy

★ Challenge Yourself ★

Challenge Words

misery	**scheme**
soggy	**cemetery**

What do you think each Challenge Word means? Check a dictionary to see if you are right. Then use separate paper to write sentences showing that you understand the meaning of each Challenge Word.

17. A headache can cause **misery**.

18. The children had a **scheme** for raising money to buy a gift.

19. Mia changed her **soggy** clothes after she fell in a puddle.

20. Some grave markers in this **cemetery** are very old.

Name: _____   Date: _____

Lesson 9

Words with Short *u*

mother

1. *u* Words
_____
_____
_____
_____
_____
_____
_____

2. *o* Words
_____
_____
_____
_____
_____
_____
_____
_____

3. *oe* Word
_____

from
Sunday
money
under
nothing
summer
does
mother
lunch
month
such
front
much
sun
other
Monday

Say and Listen
Say each spelling word. Listen for the short *u* sound.

Think and Sort
Look at the letters in each word. Think about how short *u* is spelled. Spell each word aloud.

Short *u* can be shown as /ŭ/. How many spelling patterns for /ŭ/ do you see?

1. Write the seven spelling words that have the *u* pattern.

2. Write the eight spelling words that have the *o* pattern.

3. Write the one spelling word that has the *oe* pattern.

Use the steps on page 4 to study words that are hard for you.

Spelling Patterns

u	**o**	**oe**
s**u**n	m**o**nth	d**oe**s

www.harcourtschoolsupply.com
38
Lesson 9: Words with Short *u*
Core Skills Spelling 3, SV 9781419034077

Spelling and Meaning

Letter Scramble Unscramble the underlined letters to make a spelling word. Write the word on the line.

1. When <u>osde</u> the bus come? _____
2. We hid the keys <u>drune</u> the mat. _____
3. How much <u>noemy</u> is in your pocket? _____
4. We had never seen <u>chus</u> a mess. _____
5. We could see <u>honnitg</u> in the dark. _____
6. Kelly was at the <u>tronf</u> of the line. _____

Clues Write the spelling word for each clue.

7. The first one is January. _____
8. This day comes before Tuesday. _____
9. This word is the opposite of *to*. _____
10. When it shines, you feel warmer. _____
11. This day comes after Saturday. _____
12. This person has at least one son or daughter. _____
13. If you have this, you have a lot. _____
14. This season contains June, July, and August. _____
15. This word means "different." _____

Word Story You probably use this spelling word every day. It comes from the old English word *nuncheon*, which meant "a light meal." Later *nuncheon* changed to *luncheon* and also meant "a thick piece." The spelling word names the meal you eat at noon. Write the word.

16. _____

Family Tree: does *Does* is a form of *do*. Think about how the *do* words are alike in spelling and meaning. Then add another *do* word to the tree.

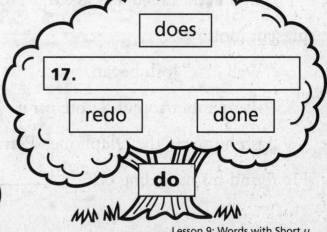

does

17. _____

redo   done

do

Lesson 9: Words with Short *u*
Core Skills Spelling 3, SV 9781419034077

Spelling in Context

Use each spelling word once to complete the story.

Facing the Music

It was June, the last _____ 1

of school. It was also the last weekend before

_____ 2 vacation. Josh's favorite day

was _____ 3 , but not this Sunday.

On Saturday Josh found ten dollars in his jacket. He could not remember

where the _____ 4 came _____ 5 . But he knew

how _____ 6 he wanted a compact disc, so he bought it with

the money.

This morning he remembered how he got the money. The ten dollars

was class money. The _____ 7 students had given him the money

to buy a present for Mr. Farar, their music teacher. Josh didn't have any more

money, and the compact disc had been on sale. He couldn't return it.

Josh was upset. His _____ 8 asked what was wrong. "It's

_____ 9 ," he told her. He couldn't bring himself to tell her about

his mistake.

Then Petra called and asked, "How _____ 10 Mr. Farar's

present look?"

"Well . . . ," Josh began.

"Remember to put a note on it. Don't forget all of our names."

Josh hung up the telephone. Petra's words had given him a great idea.

He found his modeling clay _____ 11 his bed. He formed the

clay into an egg shape and stuck a stick into it. Josh dried

the whole thing outside in the _____. Then

he painted it silver. When the paint was dry, he added all the

students' names.

By _____ morning all the names were dry.

Josh wrapped the gift and took it to school. At noon he went

to _____. Petra asked, "Where are the present

and the note?"

"You'll see," said Josh.

Mr. Farar opened his gift in _____ of

the class. "Wow! A compact disc and a silver music note

with your names on it!" he exclaimed. "This note took

_____ a lot of work. Thank you! It's one note

I'll hold forever!"

from
Sunday
money
under
nothing
summer
does
mother
lunch
month
such
front
much
sun
other
Monday

★ Challenge Yourself ★

Challenge Words

huddle
buzzard
somebody
frontier

Write the Challenge Word for each clue. Check a
dictionary to see if you are right. Then use separate
paper to write sentences showing that you
understand the meaning of each Challenge Word.

17. We use this word to talk about a person we
don't know. _____

18. This is a large bird with a beak. _____

19. This is a place where few people live. _____

20. Football players make one of these to plan their next move.

_____

Lesson 10

Contractions

they'll

1. will Contractions

_____
_____
_____
_____
_____

2. have Contractions

_____
_____
_____
_____

3. would or had Contractions

_____
_____
_____

4. is or has Contractions

_____
_____
_____

5. am Contraction

_____

she's
they'll
I've
you'll
we've
I'm
I'll
you've
it's
I'd
you'd
we'll
they'd
she'll
they've
he's

Say and Listen

Say the spelling words. Listen to the ending sounds.

Think and Sort

Each spelling word is a **contraction**. Two words are joined, but one or more letters are left out. An apostrophe (') is used in place of the missing letters.

Had and _would_ are written the same way in contractions. So are _is_ and _has_.

1. Write the five spelling words that are _will_ contractions.

2. Write the four spelling words that are _have_ contractions.

3. Write the three spelling words that are _would_ or _had_ contractions.

4. Write the three spelling words that are _is_ or _has_ contractions.

5. Write the one spelling word that is an _am_ contraction.

Use the steps on page 4 to study words that are hard for you.

Spelling Patterns

will	have	would/had	is/has	am
we'**ll**	you'**ve**	they'**d**	she'**s**	I'**m**

Spelling and Meaning

Trading Places Write the contraction that could be used instead of the underlined words in each sentence.

1. <u>It is</u> time to eat. _____
2. <u>I have</u> seen the world's tallest building. _____
3. <u>He is</u> feeling tired. _____
4. <u>You will</u> like my uncle's farm. _____
5. <u>You have</u> grown so tall! _____
6. <u>They would</u> be happy to see you. _____
7. <u>They have</u> found their ball. _____
8. <u>We will</u> make dinner together. _____
9. <u>We have</u> finished painting. _____

Rhymes Write the spelling word that completes each sentence and rhymes with the underlined word.

10. A <u>dime</u> is what _____ looking for.
11. Did you hear Kara <u>sneeze</u>? _____ got a cold.
12. If the children see a <u>whale</u>, _____ be excited.
13. The <u>seal</u> is hungry, so _____ feed it.
14. Let's buy <u>food</u> that _____ like to eat.
15. While you <u>nap</u>, _____ read a book.

Word Story Verbs have different forms for present, past, and future action. Long ago English verbs had even more forms. A few of these forms are still used today. A special form of the verb *will* used to be spelled *wolde*. Think about how we spell *wolde* today. Then add *I* and write the contraction below.

16. _____

Family Tree: *will* Think about how the *will* contractions are alike in spelling and meaning. Then add another *will* contraction to the tree.

she'll	we'll

17. _____

I'll	you'll	they'll

will

Lesson 10: Contractions
Core Skills Spelling 3, SV 9781419034077

Spelling in Context

Use each spelling word once to complete the story.

Diary of a Detective: Case 13

I went over to Riley's house to play. The first thing he did was show me some pork chops. "Look what we are having for dinner," he said with a grin.

I know Riley. _____ always hungry. I'm not.
                              1
_____ rather work on a mystery than eat.
        2

Riley's dad was next door with Mr. Sperry. Riley and I were playing in the back yard. A loud bang came from Riley's house. "_____
                                                                        3
sure that's not Mom," Riley said to me. "I know _____ still at
                                                        4
work. _____ be home in an hour."
              5

Riley and I ran to the house. The back door was wide open. A chair in the kitchen lay on its side. We walked into the hallway. "Look at my coat," I said. "_____ on the floor!" Then we heard a strange
                  6
noise upstairs.

"Let's call the police," Riley whispered to me. "_____
                                                                7
know what to do. _____ handled lots of burglars."
                        8

I didn't think it was burglars because _____ be quiet.
                                                9
Then I noticed something. "_____ got it!" I yelled.
                                  10

"Shh!" said Riley. "Be quiet, or _____ scare them off!"
                                          11

"Together _____ be able to handle this," I

said. "_____ got all the clues we need. Look

13

around."

Riley looked. Then he said, "Some of the pork chops are

gone! What burglars would take pork chops? And where did

those paw prints come from?"

Before I could answer, a puppy came down the stairs. He

barked at us.

Riley laughed. He said, "Well, puppy. I see that

_____ eaten half our dinner. Don't tell me

14

_____ like the rest."

15

The dog just wagged his tail. But _____

16

bet he was happy.

she's
they'll
I've
you'll
we've
I'm
I'll
you've
it's
I'd
you'd
we'll
they'd
she'll
they've
he's

★ Challenge Yourself ★

Challenge Words

would've
could've
who'll
where'd

Use a dictionary to look up each Challenge Word.
Then answer the questions. Use separate paper to
write sentences showing that you understand the
meaning of each Challenge Word.

17. Is **would've** a contraction for *would have*?

_____

18. Is **could've** a contraction for *could give*? _____

19. Is **who'll** a contraction for *who all*? _____

20. Is **where'd** a contraction for *where did*? _____

Lesson 11
More Words with Short *u*

butter

Say and Listen

Say each spelling word. Listen for the short *u* sound.

Think and Sort

Look at the letters in each word. Think about how short *u* is spelled. Spell each word aloud.

Short *u* can be shown as /ŭ/. How many spelling patterns for /ŭ/ do you see?

1. Write the seven spelling words that have the *u* pattern.

2. Write the two spelling words that have the *o* pattern.

3. Write the seven spelling words that have the o-consonant-e pattern.

1. *u* Words

_____
_____
_____
_____
_____
_____
_____

2. *o* Words

_____
_____

3. *o*-consonant-e Words

_____
_____
_____
_____
_____
_____
_____

lovely
just
something
hundred
done
some
sum
must
shove
won
butter
cover
supper
none
number
one

Use the steps on page 4 to study words that are hard for you.

Spelling Patterns

u	**o**	**o-consonant-e**
m**u**st	w**o**n	s**o**m**e**
	c**o**ver	

www.harcourtschoolsupply.com
46
Lesson 11: More Words with Short *u*
Core Skills Spelling 3, SV 9781419034077

Name: _____ Date: _____

Spelling and Meaning

Definitions Write the spelling word for each definition. Use a dictionary if you need to.

1. gained a victory _____
2. to put or lay over _____
3. a particular thing that is not named _____
4. a certain number of _____
5. the answer for an addition problem _____
6. a number, written 1 _____
7. ten groups of ten _____
8. will have to _____
9. amount _____
10. not any _____

Synonyms Complete each sentence by writing the spelling word that is a synonym for the underlined word.

11. Tan's work will soon be <u>finished</u>. _____
12. Tasha is wearing a <u>beautiful</u> scarf. _____
13. I'll <u>push</u> Mother's surprise in the closet. _____
14. No one could argue with the <u>fair</u> law. _____
15. Kevin ate fish and rice for <u>dinner</u>. _____

Word Story Long ago the Greek language had the word *boutyron*. *Bous* meant "cow." *Tyros* meant "cheese." The first English spelling of the word was *butere*. Write the spelling that we use today.

16. _____

Family Tree: *cover* Think about how the *cover* words are alike in spelling and meaning. Then add another *cover* word to the tree.

covering

17.

discover   covers

cover

Lesson 11: More Words with Short *u*
Core Skills Spelling 3, SV 9781419034077

Spelling in Context

Use each spelling word once to complete the story.

The First Horse Show

Simon rubbed his eyes and then looked out his bedroom window. "What a _____ day," he thought.
1

"Simon, you _____ get up now. We will be late for the show if you don't," his father called. "We've got a long way to drive, and we won't be back until it's time for _____."
2

_____."
3

Simon began to feel funny. It felt as though _____ was in his throat. He heard his father walking toward his room. He pulled the blanket up to _____ his head.
4

5

"Simon, why aren't you up yet?" his father asked.

"I _____ don't think I can do it," Simon replied.
6

"Sure you can," his father said. He smiled and gave Simon a gentle _____. "Everyone is scared before a show. Even after a _____ shows, you'll still feel that way."
7

8

Dad could always get Simon going. Simon dressed, grabbed a piece of warm toast, and spread some _____ on it.
9

Ryan watched his brother. "I want _____ toast, too," he said. Ryan placed two slices of bread in the toaster. He was seven, and he wanted to do everything Simon did.
10

Simon, his dad, and Ryan loaded their truck and began the trip to the show. For Simon the three-hour trip flew by. After they arrived at the busy arena, Simon signed in. He would be rider _____ ten. "Ten is a great number," he
11
said to himself. "It's the _____ of nine, my age,
12
and _____, for first place."
13

Simon got on his pony, Rocket. They entered the big riding ring. Simon took a deep breath. He and Rocket went to work.

As he finished the jumping course, Simon hoped that _____ of the others had _____
14   15
as well as he and Rocket had.

Simon was still holding his breath when he heard the judge say, "In first place, Simon, riding Rocket."

"Rocket, we _____!" Simon whispered to
16
his horse. "We really won!"

Word List
lovely
just
something
hundred
done
some
sum
must
shove
won
butter
cover
supper
none
number
one

★ Challenge Yourself ★

What do you think each Challenge Word means? Check a dictionary to see if you are right. Then use separate paper to write sentences showing that you understand the meaning of each Challenge Word.

Challenge Words	
income	slump
smudge	instruct

17. My allowance is my **income**.
18. The puppy's wet nose left a **smudge** on the window.
19. You will look taller if you don't **slump**.
20. I have a good teacher to **instruct** me in math.

Lesson 12

Words with Short *i*

river

Say and Listen

Say each spelling word. Listen for the short *i* sound.

Think and Sort

Look at the letters in each word. Think about how short *i* is spelled. Spell each word aloud.

Short *i* can be shown as /ĭ/. How many spelling patterns for /ĭ/ do you see?

1. Write the eleven spelling words that have the *i* pattern.

2. Write the two spelling words that have the *e* pattern.

3. Write the one spelling word that has the *e* and the *i* patterns.

4. Write the one spelling word that has the *ui* pattern.

5. Write the one spelling word that has the *ee* pattern.

1. *i* Words

_____
_____
_____
_____
_____
_____
_____
_____
_____
_____
_____

2. *e* Words

_____
_____

3. *e* and *i* Word

_____

4. *ui* Word

_____

5. *ee* Word

_____

thing
little
winter
kick
begin
river
been
dish
fill
think
spring
pretty
which
December
build
children

> Use the steps on page 4 to study words that are hard for you.

Spelling Patterns

i d**i**sh	**e** pr**e**tty	**ui** b**ui**ld	**ee** b**ee**n

Spelling and Meaning

Clues Write the spelling word for each clue.

1. what you do to a soccer ball   _____
2. young people   _____
3. what you do with a hammer and nails   _____
4. a big stream   _____
5. a season that can be cold   _____
6. a word that rhymes with *fish*   _____
7. the opposite of *end*   _____
8. a word for *beautiful*   _____
9. the opposite of *big*   _____

Rhymes Write the spelling word that completes each sentence and rhymes with the underlined word.

10. I _____ I will wear my pink shirt.
11. The coach told the player _____ pitch was good.
12. If you have not _____ practicing, you will not win the music contest.
13. I will bring you flowers in the _____.
14. Jill will climb the hill and _____ the bucket.
15. Bring that little blue _____ to me.

Word Story   The Romans of long ago divided the year into ten months. The last Roman month was named *Decem*. *Decem* meant "ten." Write the spelling word that comes from *Decem*.

16. _____

Family Tree: *children*   *Children* is a form of *child*. Think about how the *child* words are alike in spelling and meaning. Then add another *child* word to the tree.

- childlike
- 17.
- children   childproof

child

Spelling in Context

Use each spelling word once to complete the selection.

Westward Adventures

Helen Scott and her family were pioneers. They traveled west across North America when Helen was only 11 years old. Helen and other pioneers wrote about their adventures in journals, some of _____ we can

read today. Their writings have _____ helpful because they tell

us about life on the westward trail in the 1800s.

Pioneers traveled west in covered wagons. If a family lived in the middle of the country, the best time to

_____ their trip

was in the _____, after

the rains. The trip took 5 to 6

months. A family that left in

May could plan to arrive

well before the month of

_____, when

the harsh _____ began.

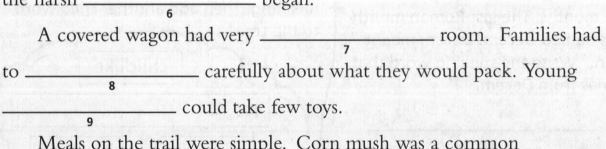

A covered wagon had very _____ room. Families had

to _____ carefully about what they would pack. Young

_____ could take few toys.

Meals on the trail were simple. Corn mush was a common

_____ that most pioneers ate. They also ate dried meat, eggs,

and potatoes.

Before dinner, pioneers gathered sticks and branches to

_____ a fire for cooking. After dinner, they
11

sang songs around the fire and danced to _____
12

fiddle music. They told stories, too.

Horses and mules pulled the wagons. The ride was bumpy

and uncomfortable. Children often walked beside the slow

wagons. They had to be careful. They didn't want the animals

to bite or _____ them.
13

Children worked on the trail, too. Boys and girls

helped get the wagons ready to cross any stream or

_____. Another _____
14   15

children did was to help make a special wax paste to

_____ cracks in the covered wagons. Then they
16

helped to fill the openings to make the wagons waterproof.

Every day on the westward trail was an adventure. Thanks

to children like Helen Scott, we can share those adventures.

| thing |
| little |
| winter |
| kick |
| begin |
| river |
| been |
| dish |
| fill |
| think |
| spring |
| pretty |
| which |
| December |
| build |
| children |

★ Challenge Yourself ★

Challenge Words

| spinach | luggage |
| width | arctic |

Write the Challenge Word for each clue. Check a
dictionary to see if you are right. Then use separate
paper to write sentences showing that you
understand the meaning of each Challenge Word.

17. This word describes very cold air. _____

18. It is a green vegetable. _____

19. This can hold your clothes when you travel. _____

20. It is the distance from one side to another. _____

Lesson 13

Words with Long *i*

lion

1. *i*-consonant-*e* Words
_____
_____
_____
_____
_____
_____
_____
_____
_____
_____
_____
_____
_____

2. *i* Words
_____
_____

3. *eye* Word
_____

alike
while
eyes
white
line
lion
size
miles
times
nice
drive
tiny
write
inside
mine
shine

Say and Listen

Say each spelling word. Listen for the long *i* sound.

Think and Sort

Look at the letters in each word. Think about how long *i* is spelled. Spell each word aloud.

Long *i* can be shown as /ī/. How many spelling patterns for /ī/ do you see?

1. Write the thirteen spelling words that have the *i*-consonant-e pattern.

2. Write the two spelling words that have the *i* pattern.

3. Write the one spelling word that has the *eye* pattern.

• Use the steps
  on page 4 to
  study words
  that are hard
  for you.

Spelling Patterns

i-consonant-**e**	**i**	**eye**
n**i**c**e**	t**i**ny	**eye** **eye**s

Spelling and Meaning

Clues Write the spelling word for each clue.

1. what people do with a car _____
2. belongs in a group with *feet* and *yards* _____
3. something that can be straight or crooked _____
4. a word meaning "at the same time" _____
5. a word that rhymes with *eyes* _____
6. what people do to some shoes _____

Analogies Write the spelling word that completes each analogy.

7. *Mean* is to _____ as *weak* is to *strong*.
8. *You* is to *me* as *yours* is to _____.
9. *Add* is to *plus* as *multiply* is to _____.
10. *Light* is to *dark* as _____ is to *black*.
11. *Hear* is to *ears* as *see* is to _____.
12. *Needle* is to *sew* as *pen* is to _____.
13. *Small* is to _____ as *big* is to *huge*.
14. *Different* is to *unlike* as *same* is to _____.
15. *Up* is to *down* as _____ is to *outside*.

Word Story One of the spelling words comes from the Greek word *leon*. *Leon* was the word for one of the big cats. The names Leona, Lenore, Leo, Leopold, and Lionel all come from this word. Write the spelling word that comes from *leon*.

16. _____

Family Tree: *drive* Think about how the *drive* words are alike in spelling and meaning. Then add another *drive* word to the tree.

driven

17.

driver   drives

drive

Name: _____ Date: _____

Spelling in Context

Use each spelling word once to complete the selection.

Just a Big Cat?

It's easy to tell that

a _____
    1

belongs to the cat family.

A lion looks very much

like a house cat. The

two animals are also

_____ in
    2

other ways. They both have

claws that they can pull

_____ their paws to keep the claws _____ and
    3   4

sharp. Lions and house cats also have _____ that see well in
                                            5

the dark. If a light should _____ on their eyes at night, their
                                6

eyes will glow.

Lions are not like house cats in every way. The greatest difference

is _____. A male lion can weigh more than 500 pounds,
    7

_____ a house cat usually weighs about 10 pounds. A house
    8

cat seems _____ next to a lion.
              9

Most lions have brownish-yellow fur. This color makes it easy for the

lion to hide. House cats come in many colors. Their fur can even be snowy

_____. The male lion has a mane. The mane makes him look
    10

big and strong. The thick mane may be why the male lion is called the king of beasts. A male house cat never has a mane.

Lions live in groups called prides. At _____, 11 as many as 35 lions may live in a pride. These lions hunt together. They may travel many _____ to 12 find food. A lion doesn't let strange animals hunt on its land. The lion will let out a roar as if to say, "Keep out! This land is _____." 13

Today most lions live in Africa, but you can still learn a lot about them. Lions can be seen in many parks and zoos. Many people will _____ a long way and stand 14 in a long _____ to see a lion. You can also read 15 books that people _____ about lions. You can 16 learn how lions live and why they are much more than big house cats.

Word List
alike
while
eyes
white
line
lion
size
miles
times
nice
drive
tiny
write
inside
mine
shine

★ Challenge Yourself ★

Challenge Words
variety   admire
chime   define

Use a dictionary to answer these questions. Then use separate paper to write sentences showing that you understand the meaning of each Challenge Word.

17. Would you find a **variety** of toys in a toy store? _____
18. Would most people **admire** a mud puddle? _____
19. Do police cars and fire trucks have sirens that **chime**? _____
20. Does a dictionary **define** words? _____

Lesson 14

More Words with Long *i*

light

1. *i* Words
_____
_____
_____
_____

2. *y* Words
_____
_____
_____
_____
_____

3. *igh* Words
_____
_____
_____

4. *uy* Word
_____

buy
Friday
fly
kind
why
child
mind
try
behind
sky
cry
high
right
by
light
night

Say and Listen
Say each spelling word. Listen for the long *i* sound.

Think and Sort
Look at the letters in each word. Think about how long *i* is spelled. Spell each word aloud.

Long *i* can be shown as /ī/. How many spelling patterns for /ī/ do you see?

1. Write the five spelling words that have the *i* pattern.

2. Write the six spelling words that have the *y* pattern.

3. Look at the word *high*. The spelling pattern for this word is *igh*. Write the four spelling words that have the *igh* pattern.

4. Write the one spelling word that has the *uy* pattern.

> Use the steps on page 4 to study words that are hard for you.

Spelling Patterns

i	y	igh	uy
k**i**nd	tr**y**	h**igh**	b**uy**

Spelling and Meaning

Definitions Write the spelling word for each definition. Use a dictionary if you need to.

1. at the back of   _____
2. to move through the air _____
3. day before Saturday   _____
4. helpful   _____
5. next to   _____

Rhymes Write the spelling word that completes each sentence and rhymes with the underlined word.

6. My _____ shoe feels too <u>tight</u>.
7. The big box of toys was <u>quite</u> _____.
8. The <u>spy</u> climbed _____ in the tree.
9. The young _____ chose a book about <u>wild</u> animals.
10. Wet or <u>dry</u>, these onions make me _____.
11. Turn on the <u>light</u> to see at _____.
12. Here's a fork so you can _____ my apple <u>pie</u>.
13. What should I _____ my mom for her birthday?
14. Do you _____ if I close the <u>blind</u>?
15. Tell me _____ you used purple <u>dye</u>.

Word Story   One spelling word comes from the Old English word *sceo*. *Sceo* meant "cloud." The spelling word names the place where we see clouds. Write the word.

16. _____

Family Tree: *light* Think about how the *light* words are alike in spelling and meaning. Then add another *light* word to the tree.

lights

17. _____

lightly   lighten

light

Spelling in Context

Use each spelling word once to complete the story.

Living Room Circus

My family and I had planned to go to the circus last _____.
1

It was a beautiful day. The sun was bright, and the _____ was
2

blue. But I got sick.

Mom made a bed for me

on the couch. Then she opened

the front door to let our cat

Tinker in. He sleeps all day in

the warm _____
3

of the sun. He plays all

_____. I
4

_____ to talk
5

Mom and Dad into letting me

stay up all night, too. If the cat

can, _____ can't
6

I? They don't agree.

Well, that day Tinker

dropped a pigeon _____ my dad's feet.
7

"Oh, no!" Mom cried. "Tinker, how could you bring that in the house?

What were you thinking?"

Mom thinks she can talk to Tinker just as she can talk to a

_____. She gets angry when Tinker acts like a cat.
8

Just then, the pigeon fluttered its wings. It wasn't hurt. It began to _____ around the room.

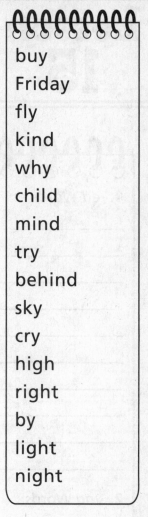

buy
Friday
fly
kind
why
child
mind
try
behind
sky
cry
high
right
by
light
night

Tinker saw the pigeon and hid _____ the couch. He jumped out as the pigeon flew by.

Mom opened the door. Tinker chased the pigeon. Dad chased Tinker. My baby brother began to _____. And I began to laugh. You couldn't _____ a ticket to a better show.

At last the pigeon flew out the door. Tinker was _____ behind it. But the pigeon got away. It flew _____ into the sky.

I was really glad that the pigeon was safe. I didn't _____ that I was sick. I got to see a circus after all! It just wasn't the _____ of circus I expected!

★ Challenge Yourself ★

Challenge Words	
designer	**glider**
cycle	**skyline**

Write the Challenge Word for each clue. Check a dictionary to see if you are right. Then use separate paper to write sentences showing that you understand the meaning of each Challenge Word.

17. It has big wings but is not a bird. _____

18. A big city has one of these. _____

19. If you ride something with wheels, you may have this. _____

20. This is a person who makes drawings and plans. _____

Lesson 15

Words with -ed or -ing

laughing

1. -ed Words

_____
_____
_____
_____
_____
_____
_____

2. -ing Words

_____
_____
_____
_____
_____
_____

ending
wished
asked
guessing
laughing
dreamed
rained
meeting
sleeping
handed
painted
filled
reading
subtracted
thanked
waited

Say and Listen

Say the spelling words. Listen for the -ed and -ing endings.

Think and Sort

Each spelling word is formed by adding -ed or -ing to a base word. A **base word** is a word from which other words are formed. The base word for *wished* is *wish*. The base word for *ending* is *end*.

Look at each spelling word. Think about the base word and the ending. Spell each word aloud.

1. Write the ten spelling words that end in -ed.

2. Write the six spelling words that end in -ing.

Use the steps on page 4 to study words that are hard for you.

Spelling Patterns

-ed	-ing
paint**ed**	read**ing**

Spelling and Meaning

Definitions Write the spelling word for each definition. Use a dictionary if you need to.

1. saw or thought during sleep   _____
2. said that one was pleased   _____
3. stayed   _____
4. a coming together for some purpose   _____
5. forming an opinion without all the facts   _____
6. passed with one's hands   _____
7. fell in drops of water from the clouds   _____

Analogies Write the spelling word that completes each analogy.

8. *Taught* is to *instructed* as *hoped* is to _____.
9. *Dress* is to *sewed* as *picture* is to _____.
10. *Playing* is to *piano* as _____ is to *book*.
11. *Chair* is to *sitting* as *bed* is to _____.
12. *Told* is to *explained* as *questioned* is to _____.
13. *Happy* is to _____ as *sad* is to *crying*.
14. *Beginning* is to *start* as _____ is to *finish*.
15. *Out* is to *emptied* as *in* is to _____.

Word Story   One of the spelling words comes from two Latin words—*sub* and *trahere*. *Sub* meant "below or away." *Trahere* meant "to pull." *Subtrahere* meant "to pull away." Write the spelling word that comes from *subtrahere*.

16. _____

Family Tree: *rained* *Rained* is a form of *rain*. Think about how the *rain* words are alike in spelling and meaning. Then add another *rain* word to the tree.

rained   rainier

17. _____

rainless

rain

Spelling in Context

Use each spelling word once to complete the story.

The Playoffs

When I left hockey practice yesterday, it was still raining. It had

_____ all day. I _____ for Dad to pick me up.
     1   **2**

Then I remembered that Mom and Dad were _____ with
                        3

teachers and other parents. They were planning our fall festival, so I walked

over to school to wait.

I tried not to think about the homework that I hadn't done yet. I had

extra math problems to do because I added numbers on our last test when I

should have _____ them. Oh, how I _____ that
        4   **5**

I had done my homework before practice. Then I would have been finished.

At school I ran into Ms. Ford, the art teacher. She was showing the

parents some pictures that students had _____. Mr. Chan, the
                   6

librarian, was also at school. I _____ him if I could wait in the
           7

library. He said yes.

I started doing my math homework. It was going pretty well. Then

Mr. Chan _____ me a book that he
     8

was sure I would like. I _____ him
         9

and looked at the cover.

The book was about my favorite hockey player,

Wayne Gretzky. It was _____ with
         10

pictures of him. I started _____.
        11

The book was great. It started with his childhood. I could hardly wait to read the _____.
12

The next thing I knew, I was on the floor, swinging my arms and yelling. Mom and Dad were there in the library. They were _____ at me. I shook my head and
13
blinked. "Was I _____?" I asked.
14

"I'm only _____," Dad said, "but I would
15
say you _____ you were a hockey player. The
16
way you were swinging your arms around, I'm glad I wasn't on the other team!"

I grinned. Too bad it was just a dream.

ending
wished
asked
guessing
laughing
dreamed
rained
meeting
sleeping
handed
painted
filled
reading
subtracted
thanked
waited

★ Challenge Yourself ★

Challenge Words

fulfilling
faltering
consented
governed

What do you think each Challenge Word means? Check a dictionary to see if you are right. Then use separate paper to write sentences showing that you understand the meaning of each Challenge Word.

17. He is **fulfilling** his promise.
18. A beginning skater may make **faltering** movements on the ice.
19. Mom **consented** to let us play.
20. The President **governed** the country for four years.

Lesson 16

Words with Short *o*

clock

1. *o* Words

_____
_____
_____
_____
_____
_____
_____
_____
_____
_____
_____
_____

2. *a* Words

_____
_____
_____

October
shop
block
bottle
o'clock
sorry
socks
problem
what
jog
wash
was
clock
bottom
forgot
body

Say and Listen

Say each spelling word. Listen for the short *o* sound.

Think and Sort

Look at the letters in each word. Think about how short *o* is spelled. Spell each word aloud.

Short *o* can be shown as /ŏ/. How many spelling patterns for /ŏ/ do you see?

1. Write the thirteen spelling words that have the *o* pattern.

2. Write the three spelling words that have the *a* pattern.

Use the steps on page 4 to study words that are hard for you.

Spelling Patterns

o	a
sh**o**p	w**a**s

Core Skills Spelling 3, SV 9781419034077

Spelling and Meaning

Clues Write the spelling word for each clue.

1. clothes that belong on your feet _____
2. has streets on all sides _____
3. in a group with *walk* and *run* _____
4. feeling regret _____
5. a question word _____
6. opposite of *remembered* _____
7. means "of the clock" _____

Analogies Write the spelling word that completes each analogy.

8. *Have* is to *has* as *were* is to _____.
9. *Month* is to _____ as *day* is to *Monday*.
10. *Bark* is to *tree* as *skin* is to _____.
11. *Top* is to _____ as *up* is to *down*.
12. *Learn* is to *school* as _____ is to *store*.
13. *Solution* is to _____ as *answer* is to *question*.
14. *Soap* is to _____ as *towel* is to *dry*.
15. *Catsup* is to _____ as *pickle* is to *jar*.

Word Story One of the spelling words names an instrument for telling time. Many years ago, the instrument contained bells to sound out passing hours. The word comes from the Latin word *clocca*, which meant "bells." Write the word.

16. _____

Family Tree: *wash* Think about how the *wash* words are alike in spelling and meaning. Then add another *wash* word to the tree.

unwashed

17.

washable   rewash

wash

Name: _____   Date: _____

The Problem with P.J.

The _____ with P.J. was that she read too many mystery
                    1
books. In September she read 15 mysteries. So far in the month of

_____, she had read 12.
          2

P.J. had told Sonya about every one of the books. Sonya

_____ tired of hearing about them and decided to let P.J. know.
          3

One afternoon when the hall _____ struck 4, P.J. started
                                        4
out on her daily two-mile _____. She went around the
                                    5
_____ and into the center of town. Then she jogged past the
          6
candy _____ and headed to the lake.
          7

As she ran by the lake, something caught her eye. It looked like a

_____ floating in the lake. She could see something white at the
          8
_____ of the bottle. It looked like a rolled-up piece of paper.
          9
She could hardly believe it. Here was her chance to solve a real mystery!

It was getting late. P.J. knew she had to be home by five

_____. She was in such a hurry to get the
       10

bottle that she _____ to be careful. SPLASH!
            11

P.J.'s _____ was soaked from head to toe. But
      12

she had the bottle. She wondered _____ the
                13

message said. P.J. opened the bottle, shook out the piece of

paper, and began to read.

    "I am _____ you had to go through all this.
           14

I'll bet your shoes and _____ are soaking wet. I
              15

hope the water will _____ away your taste for
           16

mysteries. Guess who."

    Suddenly P.J. heard a giggle. She ran over to the big oak

tree. Sonya jumped out from behind it, and both girls laughed.

This mystery had been solved!

October
shop
block
bottle
o'clock
sorry
socks
problem
what
jog
wash
was
clock
bottom
forgot
body

★ Challenge Yourself ★

Challenge Words

deposit
apologize
waffle
comment

What do you think each Challenge Word means?
Check a dictionary to see if you are right. Then use
separate paper to write sentences showing that you
understand the meaning of each Challenge Word.

17. Marie decided to **deposit** a note in the bottle.

18. You should **apologize** when you hurt someone's feelings.

19. A hot **waffle** would taste good for breakfast.

20. What **comment** did his father make about Chen's grades?

Lesson 17

Words with Long *o*

snow

Say and Listen
Say each spelling word. Listen for the long *o* sound.

Think and Sort
Look at the letters in each word. Think about how long *o* is spelled. Spell each word aloud.

Long *o* can be shown as /ō/. How many spelling patterns for /ō/ do you see?

1. Write the seven spelling words that have the o-consonant-e pattern.

2. Write the six spelling words that have the *ow* pattern.

3. Write the two spelling words that have the *oe* pattern.

4. Write the one spelling word that has the *o* pattern.

1. o-consonant-e Words
_____
_____
_____
_____
_____
_____
_____

2. ow Words
_____
_____
_____
_____
_____
_____

3. oe Words
_____
_____

4. o Word
_____

slow
whole
hope
blow
joke
wrote
show
yellow
goes
toe
alone
hole
snow
close
November
know

Use the steps on page 4 to study words that are hard for you.

Spelling Patterns

o-consonant-e	ow	oe	o
h**o**pe	sl**ow**	t**oe**	N**o**vember

Lesson 17: Words with Long *o*
Core Skills Spelling 3, SV 9781419034077

Spelling and Meaning

Definitions Write the spelling word for each definition. Use a dictionary if you need to.

1. made words with a pen _____
2. moves; travels _____
3. to wish for something _____
4. the entire amount _____
5. to be familiar with _____
6. by oneself _____

Analogies Write the spelling word that completes each analogy.

7. *Shape* is to *square* as *color* is to _____.
8. *Lose* is to *win* as _____ is to *open*.
9. *January* is to *February* as _____ is to *December*.
10. *Hand* is to *finger* as *foot* is to _____.
11. *Hot* is to *fire* as *cold* is to _____.
12. *Beat* is to *drum* as _____ is to *whistle*.
13. *Write* is to *letter* as *dig* is to _____.
14. *Rabbit* is to *fast* as *tortoise* is to _____.
15. *Day* is to *night* as _____ is to *hide*.

Word Story Long ago Latin had the word *jocus*. The French changed the word to *jogleor*, which meant "juggler." A juggler does funny things. Later the English changed *jocus* to a word that means "something funny." Write the word.

16. _____

Family Tree: *know* Think about how the *know* words are alike in spelling and meaning. Then add another *know* word to the tree.

knowledge

17. _____

known   knowingly

know

Spelling in Context

Use each spelling word once to complete the story.

What Are Friends For?

Jacob wanted to go to Salvador's house on Saturday. Salvador

_____ a note to Jacob. Salvador said he wanted to be
                1

_____. Jacob knew Salvador was sad because his dog had run
        2

away. Jacob decided to go to Salvador's house anyway.

Jacob had a plan. He would tell _____ after joke. He would
                                              3

make Salvador laugh if it took the _____ day.
                                              4

"Why did the boy _____ the door and leave his father
                          5

outside in the month of _____?" Jacob asked. Salvador didn't
                                6

answer. He stared at his dog's picture.

"Because he wanted a cold pop." Jacob laughed. Salvador didn't even smile.

Jacob asked, "What kind of nail hurts when you hit it?" Salvador didn't

look up.

"A _____ nail." Jacob smiled. Salvador didn't.
          7

Jacob tried again. "What comes after a

snowstorm?" Salvador didn't answer.

Jacob said, "_____ shovels.
                      8

Here is another one. What _____
                                      9

away when you fill it up?"

"I wish you would go away," Salvador said.

Jacob was hurt. He tried not to

_____ it. He knew Salvador was
        10

hurting, too. Jacob said, "A _____. What did

the north wind say to the west wind?"
                11

"I don't _____," answered Salvador.
              12

Jacob told him anyway. "It's time to _____."
                                                    13

"I _____ you don't have any more awful
      14

jokes," Salvador said.

Jacob gave up. He ran out the door. Salvador yelled,

"Jacob, _____ down!"
              15

Jacob tripped. He flew up in the air and landed in a pile of

bright red and _____ leaves. All Salvador could
                          16

see was Jacob's nose. Salvador laughed.

Salvador wiped his eyes and said, "Thanks for cheering

me up."

Jacob smiled and said, "That's what friends are for!"

Word list
slow
whole
hope
blow
joke
wrote
show
yellow
goes
toe
alone
hole
snow
close
November
know

★ Challenge Yourself ★

Challenge Words

console   **dome**
adobe   **rodent**

Write the Challenge Word for each clue. Check a
dictionary to see if you are right. Then use separate
paper to write sentences showing that you
understand the meaning of each Challenge Word.

17. The roof of some buildings is one of these. _____

18. A mouse is this kind of animal. _____

19. Some homes in the Southwest are made of this. _____

20. You might do this to a friend who is sad. _____

Lesson 18

More Words with Long o

comb

1. o Words

_____
_____
_____
_____
_____
_____
_____
_____
_____
_____

2. oa Words

_____
_____
_____
_____
_____

3. o and oa Word

_____

most
coat
ago
hold
hello
cocoa
open
loaf
over
comb
toast
almost
boat
both
road
gold

Say and Listen

Say each spelling word. Listen for the long o sound.

Think and Sort

Look at the letters in each word. Think about how long o is spelled. Spell each word aloud.

Long o can be shown as /ō/. How many spelling patterns for /ō/ do you see?

1. Write the ten spelling words that have the o pattern.

2. Write the five spelling words that have the oa pattern.

3. Write the one spelling word that has both the o and oa patterns.

Use the steps on page 4 to study words that are hard for you.

Spelling Patterns

o	oa
m**o**st	b**oa**t

Spelling and Meaning

Definitions Write the spelling word for each definition.
Use a dictionary if you need to.

1. to arrange the hair _____
2. a precious metal _____
3. in the past _____
4. the one as well as the other _____
5. a greeting _____
6. to keep in the hand _____
7. the greatest amount _____
8. nearly _____
9. to cause something to be no longer closed _____
10. above _____
11. bread baked in one piece _____

Classifying Write the spelling word that belongs in each group.

12. hat   scarf   gloves   _____
13. milk   eggs   cereal   _____
14. street   avenue   lane   _____
15. car   train   airplane   _____

Word Story One of the spelling words was once spelled *cacao*, but many people misspelled it. They confused the word with *coco*, the name of the tree on which coconuts grow. Write the spelling word as it is spelled today.

16. _____

Family Tree: *toast* Think about how the *toast* words are alike in spelling and meaning. Then add another *toast* word to the tree.

toasted

17. _____

toasty   toasting

toast

Spelling in Context
Use each spelling word once to complete the story.

Gold Island

We spent last week at a lake that had a tiny island in the middle of it. It was called Gold Island. A legend says that a treasure was buried there many years _____ but was

1

never found.

My sister, Jasmine, was excited about the legend. One day she packed a _____ of bread and

2

some cheese. Then she got into a small _____ and rowed to the

3

island. Jasmine was going to search every inch of it until she found the treasure.

Jasmine had been gone _____ three hours when a storm

4

came up. _____ Mom and Dad were worried. So was I.

5

Jasmine can take care of herself _____ of the time. But this

6

was the worst storm I had ever seen.

Just then Jasmine came running down the _____ to our

7

cabin. "_____!" she yelled as she came inside, dripping water

8

all _____ everything.

9

"You need to change those wet clothes and _____ your

10

hair," Dad said.

I said I would make some _____ and _____.

11   12

76

"Wait," said Jasmine. "The storm blew over a tree, and I found something interesting." She reached into her _____ pockets. "Please close your eyes and then

13

_____ out your hands." We thought she was

14

crazy. But we did it. Jasmine put rocks into our hands.

"Okay," she said, "_____ your eyes."

15

The rocks looked just like _____. Then

16

Mom said, "Now I know why you are so excited. I hate to spoil your fun. These rocks only *look* like gold."

"It's easy to be fooled," Dad said. "That's why people call them fool's gold."

Jasmine hadn't found a treasure after all. But now we know another reason why the island is called Gold Island.

most
coat
ago
hold
hello
cocoa
open
loaf
over
comb
toast
almost
boat
both
road
gold

★ Challenge Yourself ★

Challenge Words
coax	solo
rodeo	patrol

Use a dictionary to answer these questions. Then use separate paper to write sentences showing that you understand the meaning of each Challenge Word.

17. Would a person **coax** cereal into a bowl? _____
18. Could one person go on a **solo** bicycle ride? _____
19. Would you find a **rodeo** in the middle of a lake? _____
20. Do police officers go on **patrol**? _____

Lesson 19

Words with /o͝o/

cook

1. *oo* Words

_____
_____
_____
_____
_____
_____
_____

2. *u*, *u*-consonant-e Words

_____
_____
_____
_____

3. *ou* Words

_____
_____
_____

book
took
cook
sure
should
stood
wood
put
poor
foot
shook
would
full
cookies
pull
could

Say and Listen

Say each spelling word. Listen for the vowel sound you hear in *book*.

Think and Sort

Look at the letters in each word. Think about how the vowel sound in *book* is spelled. Spell each word aloud.

The vowel sound in *book* can be shown as /o͝o/. How many spelling patterns for /o͝o/ do you see?

1. Write the nine spelling words that have the *oo* pattern.

2. Write the four spelling words that have the *u* or *u*-consonant-e pattern.

3. Write the three spelling words that have the *ou* pattern.

Use the steps on page 4 to study words that are hard for you.

Spelling Patterns

oo	**u**	**u**-consonant-**e**	**ou**
b**oo**k	p**u**t	s**u**re	w**ou**ld

Lesson 19: Words with /o͝o/
Core Skills Spelling 3, SV 9781419034077

Name: _____ Date: _____

Spelling and Meaning

Antonyms Write the spelling word that is an antonym of each word.

1. push   _____
2. sat   _____
3. uncertain _____
4. rich   _____
5. empty   _____
6. gave   _____

Clues Write the spelling word for each clue.

7. You put a shoe on this part of your body.   _____
8. This word means "ought to."   _____
9. Logs are made of this.   _____
10. Most people like these sweet treats.   _____
11. This word means "was able to."   _____
12. You might do this to prepare food.   _____
13. This word means "to set."   _____
14. This word sounds like *wood*.   _____
15. This word is the past tense of *shake*.   _____

Word Story Many years ago in England, people used the bark from beech trees as a kind of paper to write on. One spelling word comes from *boece*, which meant "beech." Write the word.

16. _____

Family Tree: *cook* Think about how the *cook* words are alike in spelling and meaning. Then add another *cook* word to the tree.

cooker

17. _____

cooking   cooked

cook

www.harcourtschoolsupply.com
79
Lesson 19: Words with /o͞o/
Core Skills Spelling 3, SV 9781419034077

Spelling in Context

Use each spelling word once to complete the story.

The Little Mouse

Marvin the mouse peeked over a big pile of

_____. The lion was asleep. Then

Marvin's whiskers twitched. He smelled the

chocolate _____ lying beside

the lion's _____. Marvin

wondered if he _____ try to

get one of the cookies. The little mouse was

very hungry. He decided to take the chance.

Marvin tiptoed over to the lion. He slowly reached out to

_____ the cookies toward him.

Whack! The lion _____ his big foot down on the little

mouse. Then the lion _____ up and roared. Marvin was

scared. He _____ like a leaf.

Marvin was afraid, but he was also smart. He did some fast thinking.

He said, "Mr. Lion, I'm just a _____ little mouse. You

would have to build a fire to _____ me. Are you really

_____ I would be worth the trouble?"

The lion thought about it. He was still very _____

from his last meal. The lion told Marvin to hurry away before he changed

his mind. Marvin thanked him and was gone.

80

The next day two hunters were looking for big game. They had read in a _____ that there were
13
lots of lions nearby. The hunters saw the sleeping lion. They _____ out a net and threw it over him. There
14
was nothing the lion _____ do except yell for
15
help.

Marvin heard the lion's cry. He looked until he found the lion. He said he _____ try to help. The lion
16
said, "You are too small to help."

Marvin didn't answer. He began to nibble on the net with his sharp teeth. Soon the little mouse had made a big hole. The lion slipped out of the net. He was free!

That is how the lion learned that good things often come in small packages.

book
took
cook
sure
should
stood
wood
put
poor
foot
shook
would
full
cookies
pull
could

★ Challenge Yourself ★

Challenge Words

bureau	**gourmet**
assure	**endure**

What do you think each Challenge Word means? Check a dictionary to see if you are right. Then use separate paper to write sentences showing that you understand the meaning of each Challenge Word.

17. A mouse was living in a drawer of my **bureau**.

18. It nibbled on the **gourmet** cheese Mom bought.

19. Can you **assure** me it has gone and won't come back?

20. I could not **endure** one more night of its noisy squeaks.

Lesson 20

More Words with *-ed* or *-ing*

smiling

1. Final e Dropped

_____
_____
_____
_____
_____
_____
_____
_____
_____

2. Final Consonant Doubled

_____
_____
_____
_____
_____
_____
_____

sneezed
smiling
beginning
hoped
dropping
shining
stopped
pleased
dropped
liked
taking
driving
closed
jogged
hopping
shopping

Say and Listen

Say the spelling words. Listen for the *-ed* and *-ing* endings.

Think and Sort

Each spelling word is formed by adding *-ed* or *-ing* to a base word. Look at the letters in each spelling word. Spell each word aloud. Think about how the spelling of the base word changes.

1. If a base word ends in *e*, the *e* is usually dropped before *-ed* or *-ing* is added. Write the nine spelling words in which the final *e* of the base word is dropped.

2. If a base word ends in a single vowel and a single consonant, the consonant is often doubled before *-ed* or *-ing* is added. Write the seven spelling words in which the final consonant of the base word is doubled.

Use the steps on page 4 to study words that are hard for you.

Spelling Patterns

Final e Dropped	Final Consonant Doubled
take + ing = **tak**ing	**begin** + ing = **beginn**ing

Spelling and Meaning

Synonyms Write the spelling word that is a synonym for each word.

1. trotted _____
2. starting _____
3. shut _____
4. wished _____
5. enjoyed _____
6. sparkling _____
7. quit _____
8. grinning _____
9. jumping _____

Rhymes Write the spelling word that completes each sentence and rhymes with the underlined word.

10. The singer was not <u>pleased</u> when I _____.
11. Are you _____ the cake you are <u>making</u>?
12. The bus <u>stopped</u>, and my backpack _____.
13. To turn <u>diving</u> into _____, add the letter *r*.
14. Mom was not _____ when I <u>teased</u> my brother.
15. I keep _____ the jelly and <u>mopping</u> up the mess.

Word Story Long ago in England, people sold things in places called *schoppes*. A *schoppe* was a booth in a marketplace. Write the spelling word you can make from this word plus *-ing*.

16. _____

Family Tree: *pleased* *Pleased* is a form of *please*. Think about how the *please* words are alike in spelling and meaning. Then add another *please* word to the tree.

pleased

17. _____

pleasure   unpleasant

please

Lesson 20: More Words with -ed or -ing
Core Skills Spelling 3, SV 9781419034077

Spelling in Context

Use each spelling word once to complete the selection.

Puppy Love

Have you always _____ dogs? Have you
                    1

ever _____ to own one? Suppose you have a
        2

new puppy. What do you need to know?

At the _____ of a young puppy's life, it
          3

needs three good meals a day. After it is five months old, your pup may need

only two meals a day. Feed your puppy only dog food. If you have been

_____ leftovers from your dinner plate into your puppy's dish,
    4

you should stop. People food is not always good for animals. Dogs need dog

food and lots of water.

Handle your puppy gently. Be careful. It may try to squirm and

wiggle out of your arms. Your puppy could get badly hurt if you

_____ it.
   5

Do not get in the habit of _____ your pup to bed with
                 6

you. A puppy can sleep in your bedroom, but it should stay in its own bed.

Also be sure your doors are _____ so that your puppy will not
             7

get out and hurt itself or your things at night.

Teach your puppy good manners. It should not be jumping on everyone

and _____ onto every lap. This kind of behavior must be
     8

_____. Put the puppy back on the floor. Say in a firm voice,
   9

"No, Scooter. No." Soon you will be _____ at how well your
               10

puppy behaves.

Pay attention to your puppy's health. If your pup has coughed or _____ 11 for several days, take it to a vet. Even if your pup is healthy, take it in for regular checkups and shots.

When your puppy is outdoors, keep it on a leash. A leash helps keep it away from people, other animals, and traffic. After you have played ball or _____ 12 a few blocks with your puppy, give it cool water. Let it rest for a while, too.

Get your puppy used to riding in a car. Make sure it is in its carrier while the driver is _____ 13. Also make sure someone stays with your puppy when you or a family member is _____ 14 in a store. Never leave your puppy alone in a closed car, especially when it is hot and the sun is _____ 15. This is dangerous!

Learn all you can about pet care. That way both you and your pup can keep laughing and _____ 16.

sneezed
smiling
beginning
hoped
dropping
shining
stopped
pleased
dropped
liked
taking
driving
closed
jogged
hopping
shopping

★ Challenge Yourself ★

What do you think each Challenge Word means? Check a dictionary to see if you are right. Then use separate paper to write sentences showing that you understand the meaning of each Challenge Word.

Challenge Words

jabbing
crinkled
estimated
stunned

17. I wasn't **jabbing** the window with a stick.

18. Straighten the **crinkled** paper.

19. We **estimated** that we picked up 500 cans.

20. The dog's huge size **stunned** me!

Lesson 21

Words with /o͞o/ or /yo͞o/

school

Spelling List

1. *oo* Words
_____
_____
_____
_____

2. *ue, ew* Words
_____
_____
_____
_____
_____
_____

3. *u*-consonant-*e* Words
_____
_____
_____

4. *o, o*-consonant-*e* Words
_____
_____
_____

noon
huge
few
used
tooth
blue
school
Tuesday
who
knew
two
true
too
news
move
June

Say and Listen

Say each spelling word. Listen for the vowel sound you hear in *noon* and *huge*.

Think and Sort

The vowel sound in *noon* and *huge* can be shown as /o͞o/. In *huge* and some other /o͞o/ words, *y* is pronounced before /o͞o/.

Look at the letters in each word. Think about how /o͞o/ or /yo͞o/ is spelled. Spell each word aloud.

1. Write the four spelling words with the *oo* pattern.

2. Write the six spelling words with the *ue* or *ew* pattern.

3. Write the three spelling words with the *u*-consonant-*e* pattern.

4. Write the three spelling words with the *o* or *o*-consonant-*e* pattern.

Use the steps on page 4 to study words that are hard for you.

Spelling Patterns

oo	**ue**	**ew**
n**oo**n	tr**ue**	n**ew**s
u-consonant-**e**	**o**	**o**-consonant-**e**
h**u**g**e**	wh**o**	m**o**v**e**

Spelling and Meaning

Classifying Write the spelling word that belongs in each group.

1. lunch time   twelve o'clock   _____
2. report   information   _____
3. what   where   _____
4. mouth   tongue   _____
5. wiggle   walk   _____
6. post office   library   _____
7. red   green   _____

Clues Write the spelling word for each clue.

8. one of the summer months   _____
9. not very many   _____
10. the sum of one plus one   _____
11. means the same as *also*   _____
12. gigantic   _____
13. the opposite of *false*   _____
14. not new   _____
15. sounds like *new*   _____

Word Story   The Vikings were people who came to England long ago. One spelling word comes from the word *Tiwesdaeg*. *Tiw* was the name of the Viking war god. *Daeg* meant "day." Write the spelling word that comes from *Tiwesdaeg*.

16. _____

Family Tree: *move* Think about how the *move* words are alike in spelling and meaning. Then add another *move* word to the tree.

- moveable
- 17. _____
- moving
- unmoved
- move

Spelling in Context

Use each spelling word once to complete the story.

The All-School Marathon

_____ was a perfect day for the all-school marathon.
[1]

The sun was out, but it wasn't _____ hot to run. Jesse
[2]

_____ he was in good shape. "I should be," he thought. "I've
[3]

been training all through _____, July, and August."
[4]

Jesse was new in town. He had moved to Green City late in the

_____ year. He went to his new school for only two weeks. He
[5]

didn't know anyone. He had met one boy, but it had been too hard for them

to talk. They had met at the dentist's office. The boy was having a chipped

_____ fixed while Jesse was having his teeth cleaned. Jesse had
[6]

spent the summer by himself. He had _____ the summer to get
[7]

in shape for the race.

It was almost _____ when Jesse saw the three-mile marker.
[8]

He was among the first ten runners. He was the only one of them wearing

_____ and white, the colors of his school. "If I win," he
[9]

thought, "everybody will know _____ I am."
[10]

Jesse pushed on. Only _____ runners
11

were in front of him now. He saw the finish line ahead. Then

Jesse made his _____ on the leaders. For a
12

_____ yards, they were all neck and neck.
13

Without warning, Jesse tripped. He fell and scraped his

knee. A _____ crowd gathered around him.
14

"Did I win or lose?" he asked.

"You finished second," a girl said. "But I've got some good

_____ for you. That's the first time our school
15

ever came close to winning."

"It's _____," said a boy. "You're the best
16

runner we've ever had."

Jesse looked up. It was the boy from the dentist's office.

"Remember me?" the boy asked. "My name is Jack."

Jesse smiled. He had not won the race, but he had won a

new friend!

| noon |
| huge |
| few |
| used |
| tooth |
| blue |
| school |
| Tuesday |
| who |
| knew |
| two |
| true |
| too |
| news |
| move |
| June |

★ Challenge Yourself ★

Challenge Words

pursue   **shrewd**
casual   **dispute**

Write the Challenge Word for each clue. Check a
dictionary to see if you are right. Then use separate
paper to write sentences showing that you
understand the meaning of each Challenge Word.

17. T-shirts and jeans are this type of clothing. _____

18. Your teacher can help you with this. _____

19. A clever person is this. _____

20. When you chase someone, you do this to them. _____

Lesson 22

Words with /ûr/

bird

1. ur Words

_____
_____
_____

2. ir Words

_____
_____
_____
_____
_____

3. or Words

_____
_____
_____
_____

4. ear Words

_____
_____

5. ere Word

_____

curl
world
learn
turn
were
girl
word
bird
work
earth
first
Thursday
dirt
worm
fur
third

Say and Listen

The spelling words for this lesson contain the /ûr/ sounds you hear in *curl*. Say each spelling word. Listen for the /ûr/ sounds.

Think and Sort

Look at the letters in each word. Think about how the /ûr/ sounds are spelled. Spell each word aloud. How many spelling patterns for /ûr/ do you see?

1. Write the four spelling words that have the *ur* pattern.

2. Write the five spelling words that have the *ir* pattern.

3. Write the four spelling words that have the *or* pattern.

4. Write the two spelling words that have the *ear* pattern.

5. Write the one spelling word that has the *ere* pattern.

Use the steps on page 4 to study words that are hard for you.

Spelling Patterns

ur	ir	or	ear	ere
c**ur**l	f**ir**st	w**or**k	**ear**th	w**ere**

Spelling and Meaning

Definitions Write the spelling word for each
definition. Use a dictionary if you need to.

1. a long, thin creature that crawls _____

2. a young female child _____

3. the third planet from the sun _____

4. coming at the beginning _____

5. next after second _____

6. to move around _____

7. the day between Wednesday and Friday _____

8. a group of letters that has a meaning _____

9. soil or earth _____

Synonyms Write the spelling word that is a synonym
for the underlined word in each sentence.

10. Dinosaurs <u>existed</u> on Earth long ago. _____

11. Next year I hope to <u>study</u> French. _____

12. We finished our <u>task</u> in the garden. _____

13. I will <u>loop</u> my hair around my finger. _____

14. Wouldn't it be fun to go around the <u>earth</u>? _____

15. Our dog's <u>hair</u> is thick and black. _____

Word Story Sometimes
the spelling of words changes to
make them easier to say or sound
nicer. One of the spelling words was
once spelled *brid*. Over time, people
switched the order of the *r* and *i*.
Write the spelling word that shows
how *brid* is spelled today.

16. _____

Family Tree: *work* Think about
how the *work* words are alike in spelling
and meaning. Then add another *work*
word to the tree.

works

17. _____

rework   worker

work

Spelling in Context

Use each spelling word once to complete the story.

The Bunting

Last _____ my class went to Lone Pine State Park for a
                1

nature walk. We take these trips to _____ about nature. Each
                                            2

class trip seems as though it is a holiday.

At the park a _____ named Jane said she would
                      3

be our guide. She told us that keeping the planet healthy is important

_____. We learned lots of interesting facts about the
         4

_____ and sky. Then she told us what plants and animals
         5

to look for. Jane said that we might even see a painted bunting. A painted

bunting is a rare _____ with red, blue, and green feathers.
                          6

We _____ only a little way down the trail when my friend
            7

Elissa spotted a fawn. It had white spots on its _____. If only I
                                                              8

could find something special, too!

Lesson 22: Words with /ûr/
Core Skills Spelling 3, SV 9781419034077

I kept my eyes and ears open as I walked. The path turned once, twice, and then a _____ time. I

<u>9</u>

happened to look down at the _____ beside

<u>10</u>

a tall oak tree. At _____ I saw only a wiggly

<u>11</u>

pink _____. I watched it _____

<u>12</u>   <u>13</u>

and uncurl. Then I saw one of the most beautiful things

in the _____. I saw a real live painted

<u>14</u>

bunting. I wanted to yell to the others, but I didn't say a

_____. I didn't want to scare it away.

<u>15</u>

I stood as still as a stone and watched the bird hop up to

the tree, then _____ and fly away. In a flash of

<u>16</u>

color, it was gone. No one else saw the bunting. That was all

right with me. I knew how lucky I had been.

---

curl
world
learn
turn
were
girl
word
bird
work
earth
first
Thursday
dirt
worm
fur
third

★ Challenge Yourself ★

Challenge Words

circular   **surgeon**
dessert   **flourish**

Use a dictionary to answer these questions. Then use separate paper to write sentences showing that you understand the meaning of each Challenge Word.

17. Is the trunk of a pine tree **circular**? _____

18. Would you expect to see a **surgeon** in a bird's nest? _____

19. Would you expect to find grass in a **dessert**? _____

20. Do some birds **flourish** in wooded areas? _____

Lesson 23
Words with /ä/

barn

1. *a* Words
_____
_____
_____
_____
_____
_____
_____
_____
_____
_____
_____
_____
_____
_____

2. *ea* Word
_____

dark
yard
art
market
garden
hard
heart
father
March
arm
barn
start
star
card
sharp
bark

Say and Listen
Say each spelling word. Listen for the vowel sound you hear in *dark*.

Think and Sort
Look at the letters in each word. Think about how the vowel sound in *dark* is spelled. Spell each word aloud.

The vowel sound in *dark* can be shown as /ä/. How many spelling patterns for /ä/ do you see?

1. Write the fifteen spelling words that have the *a* pattern.

2. Write the one spelling word that has the *ea* pattern.

Use the steps on page 4 to study words that are hard for you.

Spelling Patterns

a	ea
d**a**rk	h**ea**rt

Spelling and Meaning

Clues Write the spelling word for each clue.

1. where flowers grow _____
2. where to buy fruits and vegetables _____
3. month after February _____
4. what you send on someone's birthday _____
5. where farm animals sleep _____
6. a place to play near a house _____
7. what the inside of a cave is _____
8. what stones are _____
9. another word for *dad* _____
10. the kind of knife you need to cut things _____
11. what the car does when Mom turns the key _____
12. a drawing or painting _____

Multiple Meanings Write the spelling word that has more than one meaning and completes each sentence below.

13. The movie _____ wished upon a shining _____.
14. My _____ pounded as I put all my _____ into the final leg of the race.
15. I heard Scooter _____ at the squirrel gnawing on the tree _____.

Word **Story** Words that are spelled alike but have different meanings are called **homographs.** One spelling word is a homograph that means "a weapon." The word is also a homograph that names a part of the body. Write the spelling word

16. _____

Family Tree: *start* Think about how the *start* words are alike in spelling and meaning. Then add another *start* word to the tree.

restart

17.

starter   starting

start

Spelling in Context

Use each spelling word once to complete the selection.

Annie Oakley

One of the great sharpshooters in Buffalo Bill's Wild West Show was Annie Oakley. Annie was born on a farm in Ohio on August 13, 1860. Annie's mother and _____ (1) had seven children. They lived in a small log cabin. The forest was their _____ (2). Annie's family shaved the _____ (3) off logs. They used the logs to make furniture.

Annie Oakley

Life on the Oakley farm was _____ (4). The family had to feed all of the animals that lived in the pens and in the _____ (5). They had to pick the vegetables they grew in their _____ (6). They could not afford to buy many things at a _____ (7). Annie learned to hunt to help feed her family. She became a sharpshooter on the family farm.

Annie put her whole _____ (8) into her work. She often practiced shooting until it was _____ (9). All her hard work helped her become a _____ (10). In 1875 Annie won a shooting contest against champion Frank E. Butler. Annie and Frank later married.

In _____ of 1884, Annie met Sitting Bull.
                11
Sitting Bull was the chief of the Sioux tribe. Sitting Bull liked

Annie's _____ eyesight and good aim. He gave
              12
her the nickname Little Sure Shot.

   Shortly after she got her nickname, Frank and Annie

joined Buffalo Bill's Wild West Show. Buffalo Bill used Annie's

sharpshooting act to _____ the show. One
                          13
of her most amazing tricks was shooting the thin edge of a

playing _____. She did this while holding a
            14
rifle with only one _____.
                          15
   Annie thought sharpshooting was more than just quick,

fancy shooting. She believed it was an _____.
                                              16

Word list (spiral notepad):
- dark
- yard
- art
- market
- garden
- hard
- heart
- father
- March
- arm
- barn
- start
- star
- card
- sharp
- bark

★ Challenge Yourself ★

Challenge Words
carton   starch
artistic   barbecue

What do you think each Challenge Word means?
Check a dictionary to see if you are right. Then use
separate paper to write sentences showing that you
understand the meaning of each Challenge Word.

17. You can buy milk in a **carton** or a jug.
18. A lot of **starch** on your shirt will make it stiff.
19. Annie Oakley thought that sharpshooting was **artistic**.
20. My sister served **barbecue** at her wedding.

Lesson 24 Words with /oi/

boil

1. oi Words

_____
_____
_____
_____
_____
_____
_____
_____
_____
_____
_____

2. oy Words

_____
_____
_____
_____
_____

coin
boy
choice
spoil
royal
boil
voice
toy
soil
joy
noise
point
broil
enjoy
join
oil

Say and Listen

Say each spelling word. Listen for the vowel sound you hear in *coin*.

Think and Sort

Look at the letters in each word. Think about how the vowel sound in *coin* is spelled. Spell each word aloud.

The vowel sound in *coin* can be shown as /oi/. How many spelling patterns for /oi/ do you see?

1. Write the eleven spelling words that have the *oi* pattern.

2. Write the five spelling words that have the *oy* pattern.

Use the steps on page 4 to study words that are hard for you.

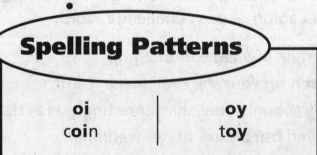

Spelling Patterns

oi	oy
c**oi**n	t**oy**

Name: _____   **Date:** _____

Spelling and Meaning

Classifying Write the spelling word that belongs in each group of words.

1. noble   kingly   _____
2. gas   coal   _____
3. doll   yo-yo   _____
4. happiness   pleasure   _____
5. sound   speech   _____
6. rot   decay   _____
7. tie   connect   _____
8. money   dollar bill   _____

Analogies Write the spelling word that completes each analogy.

9. *Man* is to *woman* as _____ is to *girl*.
10. *Laugh* is to _____ as *cry* is to *fear*.
11. *Lose* is to *loss* as *choose* is to _____.
12. *Soft* is to *whisper* as *loud* is to _____.
13. *Ocean* is to *sea* as _____ is to *dirt*.
14. *Cake* is to *bake* as *steak* is to _____.
15. *Finger* is to _____ as *hand* is to *wave*.

Word Story This spelling word tells what happens when a liquid gets very hot. It comes from the Latin word *bulla*. *Bulla* meant "bubble." When a liquid gets very hot, we can see large bubbles in it. The bubbles move around very quickly. Write the word.

16. _____

Family Tree: *joy* Think about how the *joy* words are alike in spelling and meaning. Then add another *joy* word to the tree.

enjoy

17. _____

joyful   joys

joy

Spelling in Context

Use each spelling word once to complete the story.

A Camping Tale

Liza was full of _____ when she caught the fish. But
             1

soon after that, she realized she was alone. She yelled until she almost lost her

_____. But no one answered. She was lost. There was no one
     2

to _____ the way back to camp. Her camping trip had become
       3

a nightmare.

"I might not _____ it," she thought, "but I guess I'll have to
          4

make it alone. I don't have any other _____!"
                               5

At first Liza jumped at every _____ in the woods. But
                        6

soon she got used to the noises. She was very hungry. At least she had a few

supplies in her backpack.

"The first thing I'll do," she thought, "is build a fire. It will keep me

warm. Then I'll _____ some water for cocoa. I don't have any
          7

_____ to fry the fish. But I think I can _____ it
   8   9

over the fire. I'll cook a _____ feast!"
                   10

Liza gathered wood and

put it in a little pile. She

realized she needed matches.

She put her hand in her right

pocket but found only an old

_____. Then she
  11

Lesson 24: Words with /oi/
Core Skills Spelling 3, SV 9781419034077

tried the other pocket. She found her yo-yo. "I don't think a

_____ will help me start a fire," she said aloud.
        12

She looked in her backpack. She found the matches and lit the

wood. Soon she had a little fire going.

Liza had just finished broiling the fish when it began

to rain. She didn't want the rain to _____
                                              13

her dinner. She pushed a branch into the soft

_____. Then she put her jacket over it to make
        14

a kind of tent. She ate her fish and listened to the rain. She

began to yawn and fell asleep.

When she woke up, a _____ was looking
                              15

into the tent. It was her brother. "Breakfast is ready," he said.

"Aren't you going to _____ us?"
                            16

Liza was in her family's tent. She laughed. Her nightmare

camping trip was only a dream.

coin
boy
choice
spoil
royal
boil
voice
toy
soil
joy
noise
point
broil
enjoy
join
oil

★ Challenge Yourself ★

Challenge Words

moisten
poisonous
rejoice
enjoyment

Use a dictionary to answer these questions. Then use
separate paper to write sentences showing that you
understand the meaning of each Challenge Word.

17. Do people ever **moisten** stamps?

_____

18. Are **poisonous** snakes dangerous? _____

19. Does Liza **rejoice** when she realizes she is lost? _____

20. Does a nightmare usually bring **enjoyment**? _____

Lesson 25
More Contractions

don't

1. Two Words

_____
_____
_____
_____
_____
_____
_____
_____
_____
_____
_____
_____
_____
_____

2. One Word

_____

isn't
weren't
can't
doesn't
hadn't
mustn't
wouldn't
won't
shouldn't
aren't
wasn't
don't
couldn't
didn't
hasn't
haven't

Say and Listen

Say the spelling words. Listen for the sounds at the end of each word.

Think and Sort

All of the spelling words in this lesson are contractions. Each contraction is formed from the word *not* joined with another word. When the two words are joined, one or more letters are left out. An apostrophe (') is used to show the missing letters.

In the contraction *won't*, the spelling of *will* changes to *wo*. One contraction, *can't*, is formed from one word, not two separate words.

1. Write the fifteen spelling words that are formed from *not* joined with a separate word.

2. Write the one spelling word that is formed from one word.

Use the steps on page 4 to study words that are hard for you.

Spelling Patterns

is + n**o**t	w**ill** + n**o**t	can**no**t
isn**'**t	w**o**n**'**t	can**'**t

Spelling and Meaning

Either . . . or Write the spelling word that completes each sentence.

1. Either Wags will or he _____.
2. Either you do or you _____.
3. Either James could or he _____.
4. Either Julie would or she _____.
5. Either Sara does or she _____.
6. Either Ricky was or he _____.

Trading Places Write the contraction that can be used instead of the underlined word or words in each sentence.

7. Marta <u>had not</u> seen the new puppy.   _____
8. You <u>must not</u> touch the wet paint.   _____
9. Lan <u>did not</u> bring his lunch.   _____
10. I <u>cannot</u> believe you ran five miles!   _____
11. The mail <u>has not</u> come yet.   _____
12. I <u>have not</u> finished my homework.   _____
13. Did you know that whales <u>are not</u> fish?   _____
14. We <u>were not</u> home on Saturday.   _____
15. "That <u>is not</u> my car," Ms. Ford said.   _____

Word Story One of the spelling words is a form of the word *shall*. First it was spelled *sceolde*. Then the spelling changed to *shollde*. Now it is spelled another way. Write the spelling word that is a form of this word plus *not*.

16. _____

Family Tree: *haven't* *Haven't* is a contraction of *have* and *not*. Think about how the *have* words are alike in spelling and meaning. Then add another *have* word to the tree.

having

17.

has   haven't

have

Name: _____   Date: _____

Use each spelling word once to complete the story.

The Challenge

Max watched Hector nervously, waiting to see what he would do next.

This was the first time he had faced Hector. Max _____ 1 happy

about it. "If only I _____ 2 said yes to his challenge," he thought.

"Then I _____ 3 be in this mess."

"You _____ 4 going to back down, are you?" Hector asked.

Max knew he could not back down now. He just _____ 5 .

A lot of his friends were watching him. They _____ 6 going

to leave until it was all over. They had tried to tell him about Hector.

"You _____ 7 heard?" they had asked. "He's tough. He

_____ 8 ever lose."

Max _____ 9 like to lose. His hands were sweaty. His knees

were shaking. "I _____ 10 help it," he thought. "I want to win."

Max rubbed his hands on his jeans. "Calm down," he told himself.

"Whatever happens, I

_____ 11 look

scared. I _____ 12

want to make it easy for Hector

to win. Besides, it really

_____ 13 be the end

of the world if I lose."

Then Hector made his move. Max knew that it was the wrong one. "He _____ got a chance now!" he

      14

thought. Max grinned. "You _____ have done

      15

that, Hector," he said. "I'm going to win. But don't worry. It

_____ going to hurt for long." In one move

  16

Max cleared the checkerboard of Hector's pieces. The game was over.

    Hector shook Max's hand and smiled. Max smiled back. He had met the challenge.

isn't
weren't
can't
doesn't
hadn't
mustn't
wouldn't
won't
shouldn't
aren't
wasn't
don't
couldn't
didn't
hasn't
haven't

★ Challenge Yourself ★

Challenge Words

there'll	how'd
we'd	there'd

Use a dictionary to answer these questions. Then use separate paper to write sentences showing that you understand the meaning of each Challenge Word.

17. Is **there'll** a contraction for the words *there will*?

_____

18. Is **how'd** a contraction for the words *how did*? _____

19. Is **we'd** a contraction for *we did*? _____

20. Is **there'd** a contraction for the words *there did*? _____

Lesson 26 | Words with /ô/

frog

Say and Listen

Say each spelling word. Listen for the vowel sound you hear in *draw*.

Think and Sort

Look at the letters in each word. Think about how the vowel sound in *draw* is spelled. Spell each word aloud.

The vowel sound in *draw* can be shown as /ô/. How many spelling patterns for /ô/ do you see?

1. Write the six spelling words that have the *o* pattern.

2. Write the six spelling words that have the *a* pattern.

3. Write the two spelling words that have the *ough* pattern.

4. Write the one spelling word that has the *au* pattern.

5. Write the one spelling word that has the *aw* pattern.

Use the steps on page 4 to study words that are hard for you.

Spelling list:

draw
walk
bought
because
frog
along
long
water
always
brought
off
belong
mall
strong
tall
talk

1. *o* Words
_____
_____
_____
_____
_____
_____

2. *a* Words
_____
_____
_____
_____
_____
_____

3. *ough* Words
_____
_____

4. *au* Word
_____

5. *aw* Word
_____

Spelling Patterns

o	**a**	**ough**	**au**	**aw**
l**o**ng	t**a**lk	b**ough**t	bec**au**se	dr**aw**

Lesson 26: Words with /ô/
Core Skills Spelling 3, SV 9781419034077

Spelling and Meaning

Antonyms Write the spelling word that is an antonym of each underlined word.

1. Elephants are very large and <u>weak</u>. _____
2. Please turn <u>on</u> the light. _____
3. Tina <u>never</u> eats breakfast. _____
4. That basketball player is very <u>short</u>. _____
5. Mr. Good gave a <u>brief</u> speech. _____

Clues Write the spelling word for each clue.

6. what you do on the phone _____
7. what people and animals drink _____
8. place to shop _____
9. past tense of *bring* _____
10. what artists do _____
11. green thing that sits on a lily pad _____
12. means "to be owned by" _____
13. means almost the same as *beside* _____
14. rhymes with *talk* _____
15. past tense of *buy* _____

Word Story People used to say that a dish broke "by cause" it fell. Later, they made one word of *by* and *cause*. Write the word as it is spelled today.

16. _____

Family Tree: *talk* Think about how the *talk* words are alike in spelling and meaning. Then add another *talk* word to the tree.

talkative

17. _____

talks   talker

talk

Spelling in Context

Use each spelling word once to complete the story.

The Frog Prince

Libby's older sister, Rachel, liked to

_____ pictures. One
1

day she drew a picture of a green

_____. It had a little
2

gold crown on its head. Rachel _____ the picture to Libby.
3

Rachel could not hear, so the two girls used their hands to talk to each

other. "If you find a frog, it might turn into a prince," Rachel signed to Libby

with her hands. Libby had a _____ feeling that Rachel was
4

teasing her.

"That's just silly _____," Libby signed back. But not
5

_____ after, she wondered what a frog prince would be like.
6

Would he be short or _____? Would he be kind? Libby
7

thought about what she would say to him.

"Aren't you ready yet?" Mom called. Libby's daydream ended.

Sometimes Libby's mom spent Saturday afternoon shopping at the

_____. Libby _____ went. Rachel usually
8   9

came _____, too. Today at the mall, Mom and Rachel
10

_____ a snack. Libby wanted to be by herself. She decided to
11

_____ around the mall.
12

It was warm, so Libby took _____ her jacket. She was
13

still hot. "Maybe it's cooler by the _____," she thought. Libby
14

walked to the pond in the center of the mall. She sat down on the low wall around it. Suddenly a frog jumped to the wall and sat beside her.

"Could it be a prince?" Libby wondered. As she reached for the frog, a voice yelled, "Leave that frog alone! It doesn't _____ to you!"
15

Mr. Muller, the pet store owner, rushed over. "What are you doing to my frog?" he asked. "I've been searching for him everywhere."

"Nothing at all," Libby replied. "I just wanted to help him _____ he might be . . ." She stopped. It
16
sounded so silly. She got up and quickly walked away.

"Now I'll never be sure," Libby thought as she went to look for her mom and Rachel.

draw
walk
bought
because
frog
along
long
water
always
brought
off
belong
mall
strong
tall
talk

★ Challenge Yourself ★

Challenge Words

| sausage | broth |
| dawdle | install |

Use a dictionary to answer these questions. Then use separate paper to write sentences showing that you understand the meaning of each Challenge Word.

17. Should you comb your hair with a **sausage**? _____
18. Could you find **broth** in vegetable soup? _____
19. If you were in a hurry, would you **dawdle**? _____
20. Should you **install** a stove before you turn it on? _____

Name: _____ Date: _____

Lesson 27

More Words with /ô/

storm

1. *au* Words
_____
_____

2. *o* Words
_____
_____
_____
_____
_____
_____
_____
_____
_____

3. *oo, ou* Words
_____
_____
_____
_____

4. *a* Word
_____

August
morning
four
quart
pour
popcorn
before
autumn
corner
storm
door
floor
north
born
fork
sport

Say and Listen

Say each spelling word. Listen for the first vowel sound you hear in *August* and *morning*.

Think and Sort

Look at the letters in each word. Think about how the first vowel sound in *August* and *morning* is spelled. Spell each word aloud.

The first vowel sound in *August* and *morning* can be shown as /ô/. How many spelling patterns for /ô/ do you see?

1. Write the two spelling words that have the *au* pattern.

2. Write the nine spelling words that have the *o* pattern.

3. Write the four spelling words that have the *oo* or *ou* pattern.

4. Write the one spelling word that has the *a* pattern.

Use the steps on page 4 to study words that are hard for you.

Spelling Patterns

au	o	oo	ou	a
August	m**o**rning	d**oo**r	f**ou**r	quart

Spelling and Meaning

Clues Write the spelling word for each clue.

1. snack to eat at the movies   _____
2. spoon, knife, _____   _____
3. rain or snow and lots of wind   _____
4. where the walls in a room meet   _____
5. how to get milk into a glass   _____

Analogies Write the spelling word that completes each analogy.

6. *East* is to *west* as _____ is to *south*.
7. *Summer* is to *winter* as *spring* is to _____.
8. *Evening* is to *dinner* as _____ is to *breakfast*.
9. *Cool* is to *warm* as *after* is to _____.
10. *Foot* is to *yard* as _____ is to *gallon*.
11. *Above* is to *below* as *ceiling* is to _____.
12. *Lid* is to *jar* as _____ is to *house*.
13. *One* is to *two* as *three* is to _____.
14. *Color* is to *blue* as _____ is to *hockey*.
15. *Bird* is to *hatch* as *child* is to _____.

Word Story Caesar Augustus was one of the greatest Roman emperors. *Augustus* meant "very great man." Caesar Augustus had the Romans name a month after him. This month still has his name. Write the spelling word that names this month.

16. _____

Family Tree: *north* Think about how the *north* words are alike in spelling and meaning. Then add another *north* word to the tree.

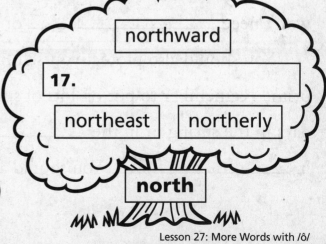

northward

17.

northeast   northerly

north

Spelling in Context

Use each spelling word once to complete the selection.

Happy Hiking

Hiking is a great _____

1

for families to enjoy together. Here are some

easy tips to make it safe and fun for everyone.

Find and wear good hiking boots.

Remember that your legs and feet will be

doing a lot of work. Break in brand new

boots _____ going hiking.

2

Wear them around on your living room

_____ first so that your feet won't hurt later.

3

Before you go out your front _____ and head for

4

the trail, make sure you pack plenty of supplies. You should also carry

water. Each person will need one _____ of water for each

5

_____ or five miles you plan to hike.

6

Pack lots of healthful snacks as well. Fruit and granola bars make good

snacks. Freshly popped and unsalted _____ is also good. You

7

won't need a _____ or spoon to eat it, either.

8

You should also protect yourself from the sun. Wear a hat with a wide

brim. Remember to put on lots of sunblock. You can get a sunburn on cool

days in the spring or in the _____ as well as on hot summer days

9

in _____. You should also take a raincoat in case rain starts to

10

_____. Remember that a _____
                11   12
can blow in at any time.

Learn how to use a compass. A compass needle always

points to the _____. Keep in mind, too, that in
                        13
the _____ the sun is always in the east. If you
              14
remember these two things, you will not get lost.

Be kind to any animals you see. Never back a wild animal

into a _____. Make noises to let animals know
              15
where you are. It is especially important to avoid disturbing

baby animals that have just been _____. Angry
                                              16
animal parents can be dangerous!

Always be sure to stay with your family and help one

another. Remembering these tips can help make your family

hiking trip the best ever!

August
morning
four
quart
pour
popcorn
before
autumn
corner
storm
door
floor
north
born
fork
sport

★ Challenge Yourself ★

Challenge Words

ornament
wharf
coarse
corridor

Write the Challenge Word for each clue. Check a dictionary to see if you are right. Then use separate paper to write sentences showing that you understand the meaning of each Challenge Word.

17. You can expect to see water and boats at this.
_____

18. You walk through this to get to another part of a building.
_____

19. This is a kind of decoration. _____

20. This word describes things that are not smooth. _____

Lesson 28
Words with /ou/

tower

1. ou Words

_____
_____
_____
_____
_____
_____
_____
_____
_____

2. ow Words

_____
_____
_____
_____
_____
_____
_____

house
flower
town
sound
ground
tower
found
brown
about
hour
power
down
around
count
our
owl

Say and Listen
Say each spelling word. Listen for the vowel sound you hear in *house*.

Think and Sort
Look at the letters in each word. Think about how the vowel sound in *house* is spelled. Spell each word aloud.

The vowel sound in *house* can be shown as /ou/. How many spelling patterns for /ou/ do you see?

1. Write the nine spelling words that have the *ou* pattern.

2. Write the seven spelling words that have the *ow* pattern.

Use the steps on page 4 to study words that are hard for you.

Spelling Patterns

ou	**ow**
h**ou**se	br**ow**n

Spelling and Meaning

Hink Pinks Hink pinks are pairs of rhyming words that have funny meanings. Read each clue. Write the spelling word that completes each hink pink.

1. a place for mice to live   mouse _____
2. a beagle's bark   hound _____
3. the time to bake   flour _____
4. rain falling on a tall building   _____ shower
5. a night bird's loud sound   _____ howl

Letter Scramble Unscramble the letters in parentheses. Then write the spelling word to complete the phrase.

6. (wodn)   run _____ the hill
7. (repow)   _____ from electricity
8. (boaut)   books for and _____ children
9. (wolfer) a _____ in a vase
10. (ungord) on the _____ or in the air
11. (dnofu) lost and _____
12. (nuoct) _____ to ten
13. (wonrb) _____ hair and eyes
14. (ruodna) in, _____, and through
15. (rou)   her, their, and _____

Word Story In Old English a fence or a wall was called a *toun*. A fence or wall became a sign that people lived nearby. The place where people lived became known as a *toun*. Write the spelling word that comes from *toun*.

16. _____

Family Tree: *power* Think about how the *power* words are alike in spelling and meaning. Then add another *power* word to the tree.

powerfully

17. _____

powerless   powers

power

Spelling in Context

Use each spelling word once to complete the selection.

Owls

Of all the birds, the

_____
                1

is one of the easiest to

recognize. An owl has

a large, round head.

It has big eyes that look

straight ahead.

Owls come in several colors. Snowy owls are white. Owls of the

deep rain forest are often dark _____ in color. At last
                                            2

_____, there were _____ 130 different kinds
            3   4

of owls. Scientists think that some owls are in danger of becoming extinct.

They feel it is _____ duty to protect them. Owls are useful to
                        5

people. They help farmers and eat rodents that hurt crops.

Owls can be _____ almost everywhere in the
                        6

world. Some owls make their home in a tree or in a barn. Some owls

have even nested on top of a water _____ near a busy
                                                7

_____.
            8

Most owls hunt for food at night. Their eyes are large, so they see well in

the dark. Owls also have very good hearing. Using their sharp hearing and

keen sight, they fly above the _____, looking for small animals
                                            9

www.harcourtschoolsupply.com
116
Lesson 28: Words with /ou/
Core Skills Spelling 3, SV 9781419034077

such as mice and rats. Owls are meat eaters. They never nibble
on leaves or the petals of a _____ .
      <u>10</u>

      An owl can swoop _____ without making
                        <u>11</u>

a _____ . Once caught, an animal has little
  <u>12</u>

chance of getting away from the _____ of the
                                <u>13</u>

owl's grip. In one _____ an owl can catch two
                   <u>14</u>

or three mice.

      Owls are as good at catching mice as cats are. But owls do

not make good _____ pets. Owls need room
              <u>15</u>

to fly _____ . The best way to enjoy owls is to
      <u>16</u>

watch them in the wild.

house
flower
town
sound
ground
tower
found
brown
about
hour
power
down
around
count
our
owl

★ Challenge Yourself ★

Challenge Words

doubtful
devour
bough
wildflower

What do you think each Challenge Word means?
Check a dictionary to see if you are right. Then use
separate paper to write sentences showing that you
understand the meaning of each Challenge Word.

17. It is **doubtful** that an owl would be a good
      house pet.

18. A hungry owl will **devour** a big meal.

19. A little owl sat on the **bough** of a tree.

20. An owl would rather eat a mouse than a **wildflower**.

Lesson 29

Words with /îr/, /âr/, or /īr/

deer

1. /îr/ Words
_____
_____
_____
_____
_____
_____
_____

2. /âr/ Words
_____
_____
_____
_____
_____
_____

3. /īr/ Words
_____
_____
_____

near
care
fire
where
hear
wire
stairs
deer
ear
year
tire
here
dear
chair
air
hair

Say and Listen

The spelling words for this lesson contain the /îr/, /âr/, and /īr/ sounds that you hear in *near*, *care*, and *fire*. Say the spelling words. Listen for the /îr/, /âr/, and /īr/ sounds.

Think and Sort

Look at the letters in each word. Think about how the /îr/, /âr/, or /īr/ sounds are spelled. Spell each word aloud.

1. Write the seven /îr/ spelling words. Underline the letters that spell /îr/ in each word.

2. Write the six /âr/ spelling words. Underline the letters that spell /âr/ in each word.

3. Write the three /īr/ spelling words. Underline the letters that spell /īr/ in each word.

Use the steps on page 4 to study words that are hard for you.

Spelling Patterns

/îr/			/âr/			/īr/
eer	**ear**	**ere**	**are**	**air**	**ere**	**ire**
d**eer**	n**ear**	h**ere**	c**are**	ch**air**	wh**ere**	f**ire**

Spelling and Meaning

Synonyms Write the spelling word that is a synonym of the underlined word.

1. Look at the long <u>fur</u> on that dog!   _____
2. These <u>steps</u> go to the attic.   _____
3. Don't trip over that <u>cord</u>.   _____
4. The Rileys are <u>loved</u> family friends.   _____

Clues Write the spelling word for each clue.

5. You breathe this.   _____
6. This animal can have antlers.   _____
7. When you listen, you do this.   _____
8. If you are concerned, you do this.   _____
9. You hear with this.   _____
10. This equals 12 months.   _____
11. This means the opposite of *far*.   _____
12. This is a question word.   _____
13. A car should have a spare one.   _____
14. Matches can start this.   _____
15. This means the opposite of *there*.   _____

Word Story   One spelling word started as the Greek word *cathedra*. *Cathedra* meant "seat." The French changed it to *chaiere*. The English changed it, too. Write the word.

16. _____

Family Tree: *near* Think about how the *near* words are alike in spelling and meaning. Then add another *near* word to the tree.

nearer

17.

nearly   nearing

near

Lesson 29: Words with /îr/, /âr/, or /ir/
Core Skills Spelling 3, SV 9781419034077

Spelling in Context

Use each spelling word once to complete the poem.

A Strange Story

Come sit _____ me,
1

My _____ children.
2

Come sit right over _____.
3

I have a little story

That I tell just once a _____.
4

Put a big log on the _____,
5

Come close to my _____.
6

And you will hear a story

That will curl all your _____.
7

Take _____ to listen closely,
8

Let me have your _____.
9

This is the strangest story

That you may ever _____!
10

I was on my way to go to bed,

I was halfway up the stairs,

When a herd of _____ came dancing down,
11

Then fourteen polar bears!

Before I could catch a breath of _____,
12

Before I could go one step higher,

What do you think went walking by?

A walrus wearing glasses made of _____.
                                              13

And it was followed by two otters

That rode in an old _____.
                              14

_____ did those animals come from?
        15

And where did all of them go?

I've asked myself a hundred times,

But still I do not know!

Some nights when it's time for bed,

And I start to climb the _____,
                                      16

I think I hear a walrus and otters

And deer and polar bears!

near
care
fire
where
hear
wire
stairs
deer
ear
year
tire
here
dear
chair
air
hair

★ Challenge Yourself ★

Challenge Words

careless **dreary**

dairy **inspire**

Write the Challenge Word for each clue. Check a dictionary to see if you are right. Then use separate paper to write sentences showing that you understand the meaning of each Challenge Word.

17. A beautiful sunset can often do this to an artist. _____

18. Cows are found at this. _____

19. If you do not pay attention to what you do, you are this.

_____

20. If a day is dark and cloudy, you can use this word to describe it.

_____

Name: _____   Date: _____

Lesson 30
Words with -er or -est

tall, taller, tallest

Say and Listen
Say each spelling word. Listen for the ending sounds.

Think and Sort
All of the spelling words end in *-er* or *-est*. Spell each word aloud.

Each spelling word is formed by adding *-er* or *-est* to a base word. Look at the letters of each base word.

1. No Change to Base Word

_____
_____
_____
_____
_____
_____
_____
_____
_____
_____

2. Final *y* Changed to *i*

_____
_____
_____
_____

3. Final Consonant Doubled

_____
_____

taller
tallest
longer
longest
dirtier
dirtiest
hotter
hottest
stronger
strongest
greater
greatest
funnier
funniest
sharper
sharpest

1. Write the ten spelling words that have no change in the base word.

2. Write the four spelling words in which the final *y* of the base word is changed to *i*.

3. Write the two spelling words in which the final consonant of the base word is doubled.

Use the steps on page 4 to study words that are hard for you.

Spelling Patterns

No Change to Base Word	Final **y** Changed to **i**	Final Consonant Doubled
tall**er**	funn**ier**	hot**ter**
tall**est**	funn**iest**	hot**test**

Spelling and Meaning

Antonyms Write the spelling word that is an antonym of the underlined word.

1. Turn on the fan if it gets <u>colder</u>. _____
2. I need the <u>dullest</u> knife for the steak. _____
3. An owl's eyes are <u>duller</u> than a robin's. _____
4. The <u>weakest</u> wrestler is most likely to win. _____
5. I will put the <u>cleanest</u> clothes in the wash. _____

Comparisons Write the spelling word that completes each comparison.

6. An oak tree is _____ than a person.
7. Her joke was the _____ one I ever heard.
8. Mt. Everest is the _____ mountain in the world.
9. Four is _____ than three.
10. A mile is _____ than a foot.
11. An elephant is _____ than a mouse.
12. The Nile River is the _____ river in the world.
13. Summer is usually the _____ season of the year.
14. Who is the _____ basketball player of all time?
15. I thought the joke was _____ than the riddle.

Word **Story** Two spelling words come from a word that used to be spelled *dritti*. People began to change its spelling. They made the first *i* change places with the *r*. Then they changed the final *i* to *y*. Write the spelling word that is the *-er* form of the word.

16. _____

Family Tree: *sharper* *Sharper* is a form of *sharp*. Think about how the *sharp* words are alike in spelling and meaning. Then add another *sharp* word to the tree.

sharpen

17. _____

sharpest   sharper

sharp

123

Spelling in Context
Use each spelling word once to complete the story.

Big Splash

Ana, Mara, and Ty were playing in the park. Ana said, "Wow, it's hot today!"

Ty wiped his face and said, "It's _____ than it's been all

month."

"It's the _____ it's ever been," cried Mara. She gave a sharp

whistle. Ana gave an even _____ one. But both girls had to cover

their ears. Ty's whistle was the _____ of all.

"Oh, Ty. You think you're so great," said Mara.

"You think you're _____ than anyone," cried Ana.

"Well, my whistle was the _____," boasted Ty. "But let's have

a real contest. Let's play tug-of-war."

Each one wanted to win. Mara was strong. But Ty thought he

was _____ than Mara. And Ana thought she was the

_____. You don't have to be tall to be strong. Ana wasn't

very tall. Mara was _____ than she was. And Ty was the

_____.

"Let's put this mud puddle between us," said Ty. "The loser will fall and

get dirty."

"I'll bet you'll get _____ than I will," said Mara.

"You'll be the _____ of all," cried Ana.

Ty and Mara were first. They pulled the rope for a long time. Mara and

Ana were next. They pulled for an even _____ time. Ty and

Ana were the last to play. Their tug-of-war contest was the

_____.
14

    Finally Ana pulled Ty into the mud. He fell with a big

splash. The mud flew. There were big spots on Ana's face.

Mara had mud on her sweater.

    "You may be the winner, Ana, but you sure look funny,"

said Mara.

    "No _____ than you," said Ana.
15

    Ty just sat in the puddle grinning. "And I'll bet I look the

_____ of all!" he laughed.
16

| taller |
| tallest |
| longer |
| longest |
| dirtier |
| dirtiest |
| hotter |
| hottest |
| stronger |
| strongest |
| greater |
| greatest |
| funnier |
| funniest |
| sharper |
| sharpest |

★ Challenge Yourself ★

Challenge Words

weirder   weirdest
shakier   shakiest

What do you think each Challenge Word means? Check a dictionary to see if you are right. Then use separate paper to write sentences showing that you understand the meaning of each Challenge Word.

17. Which is **weirder**—blue hair or a green face?
18. The shadows made the **weirdest** shapes on the wall.
19. The chair with the short leg is **shakier** than the other.
20. My chair is the **shakiest** of all.

Answer Key

Page 6
1. ask, matter, black, add, match, Saturday, class, apple, subtract, thank, catch, January, after, hammer, half
2. laugh

Page 7
1. add
2. matter
3. match
4. class
5. after
6. thank
7. half
8. ask
9. apple
10. subtract
11. hammer
12. black
13. laugh
14. January
15. catch
16. Saturday
17. Answers will vary; a sample answer is *thanked*.

Pages 8–9
1. hammer
2. match
3. class
4. matter
5. catch
6. January
7. thank
8. after
9. ask
10. half
11. apple
12. add
13. subtract
14. laugh
15. black
16. Saturday
17. many colors
18. yes
19. yes
20. no
Sentences will vary.

Page 10
1. page, change, face, save, ate, place, late, safe, came
2. gray, away, pay, May
3. great, break
4. April

Page 11
1. came
2. safe
3. away
4. place
5. page

6. great
7. change
8. gray
9. May
10. ate
11. break
12. pay
13. late
14. save
15. face
16. April
17. Answers will vary; a sample answer is *paying*.

Pages 12–13
1. save
2. change
3. face
4. great
5. pay
6. came
7. break
8. ate
9. page
10. gray
11. place
12. April
13. May
14. late
15. away
16. safe
17–20. Definitions and sentences will vary.

Page 14
1. rain, sail, afraid, aid, train, wait, aim, paint
2. fable, danger, table, able, paper
3. eight, weigh
4. they

Page 15
1. aid
2. afraid
3. wait
4. danger
5. able
6. table
7. eight
8. train
9. sail
10. fable
11. rain
12. they
13. weigh
14. paint
15. aim
16. paper
17. Answers will vary; a sample answer is *painting*.

Pages 16–17
1. rain
2. table
3. paper

4. eight
5. aid
6. afraid
7. able
8. aim
9. wait
10. paint
11. sail
12. train
13. they
14. danger
15. weigh
16. fable
17. yes
18. yes
19. yes
20. no
Sentences will vary.

Page 18
1. next, egg, end, help, spent, second, forget, dress, address, test
2. ready, read, head
3. again, said
4. says

Page 19
1. address
2. again
3. read
4. forget
5. spent
6. ready
7. help
8. says
9. second
10. test
11. said
12. next
13. end
14. dress
15. egg
16. head
17. Answers will vary; a sample answer is *helped*.

Pages 20–21
1. egg
2. again
3. dress
4. read
5. test
6. ready
7. address
8. spent
9. next
10. said
11. second
12. says
13. head
14. help
15. end
16. forget
17–20. Definitions and sentences will vary.

Page 22
1. tests, pages, papers, hammers, tables, clowns, paints, apples, eggs, hands, trains, places

2. dresses, classes, matches, addresses

Page 23
1. paints
2. hammers
3. apples
4. eggs
5. papers
6. pages
7. dresses
8. addresses
9. tests
10. matches
11. trains
12. hands
13. places
14. clowns
15. classes
16. tables
17. Answers will vary; a sample answer is *handed*.

Page 24–25
1. paints
2. hands
3. dresses
4. clowns
5. places
6. hammers
7. tables
8. apples
9. matches
10. eggs
11. papers
12. trains
13. tests
14. classes
15. pages
16. addresses
17. meteors
18. neckties
19. losses
20. caverns
Sentences will vary.

Page 26
1. slept, February, them, never, when, sent, kept, September, best, then, cents, Wednesday, better
2. friend
3. many
4. guess

Page 27
1. friend
2. many
3. September
4. Wednesday
5. slept
6. February
7. best
8. sent
9. when
10. then
11. kept
12. them
13. better
14. guess
15. never
16. cents

17. Answers will vary; a sample answer is *unfriendly*.

Pages 28–29
1. February
2. Wednesday
3. best
4. never
5. kept
6. slept
7. friend
8. then
9. better
10. guess
11. many
12. them
13. cents
14. sent
15. when
16. September
17. blend
18. friendliness
19. index
20. sketch
Sentences will vary.

Page 30
1. street, free, wheel, queen, sneeze, meet, need, sleep
2. please, read, each, team, sea, dream, meat
3. people

Page 31
1. sleep
2. street
3. people
4. sneeze
5. read
6. wheel
7. sea
8. meat
9. team
10. dream
11. meet
12. free
13. please
14. each
15. need
16. queen
17. Answers will vary; a sample answer is *reading*.

Pages 32–33
1. sea
2. queen
3. people
4. read
5. meet
6. meat
7. sleep
8. dream
9. need
10. Please
11. street
12. wheel
13. free
14. sneeze
15. team
16. each
17–20. Definitions and sentences will vary.

Page 34
1. even
2. only, story, family, sleepy, carry, sunny, funny, very, every, city, penny, happy, busy
3. these
4. key

Page 35
1. carry
2. very
3. key
4. funny
5. every
6. penny
7. these
8. story
9. only
10. happy
11. sunny
12. busy
13. city
14. sleepy
15. even
16. family
17. Answers will vary; a sample answer is *unhappy*.

Pages 36–37
1. city
2. family
3. penny
4. happy
5. sunny
6. sleepy
7. very
8. carry
9. only
10. every
11. even
12. these
13. key
14. story
15. busy
16. funny
17–20. Definitions and sentences will vary.

Page 38
1. Sunday, under, summer, lunch, such, much, sun
2. from, money, nothing, mother, month, front, other, Monday
3. does

Page 39
1. does
2. under
3. money
4. such
5. nothing
6. front
7. month
8. Monday
9. from
10. sun
11. Sunday
12. mother
13. much
14. summer
15. other

16. lunch
17. Answers will vary; a sample answer is *did*.

Pages 40–41
1. month
2. summer
3. Sunday
4. money
5. from
6. much
7. other
8. mother
9. nothing
10. does
11. under
12. sun
13. Monday
14. lunch
15. front
16. such
17. somebody
18. buzzard
19. frontier
20. huddle
Sentences will vary.

Page 42
1. they'll, you'll, I'll, we'll, she'll
2. I've, we've, you've, they've
3. I'd, you'd, they'd
4. she's, it's, he's
5. I'm

Page 43
1. It's
2. I've
3. He's
4. You'll
5. You've
6. They'd
7. They've
8. We'll
9. We've
10. I'm
11. She's
12. they'll
13. we'll
14. you'd
15. I'll
16. I'd
17. Answers will vary; a sample answer is *he'll*.

Pages 44–45
1. He's
2. I'd
3. I'm
4. she's
5. She'll
6. It's
7. They'll
8. They've
9. they'd
10. I've
11. you'll
12. we'll
13. We've
14. you've
15. you'd
16. I'll
17. yes
18. no
19. no

Core Skills Spelling 3, SV 9781419034077

20. yes
Sentences will vary.

Page 46
1. just, hundred, sum, must, butter, supper, number
2. won, cover
3. lovely, something, done, some, shove, none, one

Page 47
1. won
2. cover
3. something
4. some
5. sum
6. one
7. hundred
8. must
9. number
10. none
11. done
12. lovely
13. shove
14. just
15. supper
16. butter
17. Answers will vary; a sample answer is *uncover*.

Pages 48–49
1. lovely
2. must
3. supper
4. something
5. cover
6. just
7. shove
8. hundred
9. butter
10. some
11. number
12. sum
13. one
14. none
15. done
16. won
17–20. Definitions and sentences will vary.

Page 50
1. thing, little, winter, kick, river, dish, fill, think, spring, which, children
2. pretty, December
3. begin
4. build
5. been

Page 51
1. kick
2. children
3. build
4. river
5. winter
6. dish
7. begin
8. pretty
9. little
10. think

11. which
12. been
13. spring
14. fill
15. thing
16. December
17. Answers will vary; a sample answer is *childish*.

Pages 52–53
1. which
2. been
3. begin
4. spring
5. December
6. winter
7. little
8. think
9. children
10. dish
11. build
12. pretty
13. kick
14. river
15. thing
16. fill
17. arctic
18. spinach
19. luggage
20. width
Sentences will vary.

Page 54
1. alike, while, white, line, size, miles, times, nice, drive, write, inside, mine, shine
2. lion, tiny
3. eyes

Page 55
1. drive
2. miles
3. line
4. while
5. size
6. shine
7. nice
8. mine
9. times
10. white
11. eyes
12. write
13. tiny
14. alike
15. inside
16. lion
17. Answers will vary; a sample answer is *driving*.

Pages 56–57
1. lion
2. alike
3. inside
4. nice
5. eyes
6. shine
7. size
8. while
9. tiny
10. white
11. times
12. miles
13. mine

14. drive
15. line
16. write
17. yes
18. no
19. no
20. yes
Sentences will vary.

Page 58
1. Friday, kind, child, mind, behind
2. fly, why, try, sky, cry, by
3. high, right, light, night
4. buy

Page 59
1. behind
2. fly
3. Friday
4. kind
5. by
6. right
7. light
8. high
9. child
10. cry
11. night
12. try
13. buy
14. mind
15. why
16. sky
17. Answers will vary; a sample answer is *lighting*.

Pages 60–61
1. Friday
2. sky
3. light
4. night
5. try
6. why
7. by
8. child
9. fly
10. behind
11. cry
12. buy
13. right
14. high
15. mind
16. kind
17. glider
18. skyline
19. cycle
20. designer
Sentences will vary.

Page 62
1. wished, asked, dreamed, rained, handed, painted, filled, subtracted, thanked, waited
2. ending, guessing, laughing, meeting, sleeping, reading

Page 63
1. dreamed
2. thanked

3. waited
4. meeting
5. guessing
6. handed
7. rained
8. wished
9. painted
10. reading
11. sleeping
12. asked
13. laughing
14. ending
15. filled
16. subtracted
17. Answers will vary; a sample answer is *rainy*.

Pages 64–65
1. rained
2. waited
3. meeting
4. subtracted
5. wished
6. painted
7. asked
8. handed
9. thanked
10. filled
11. reading
12. ending
13. laughing
14. sleeping
15. guessing
16. dreamed
17–20. Definitions and sentences will vary.

Page 66
1. October, shop, block, bottle, o'clock, sorry, socks, problem, jog, clock, bottom, forgot, body
2. what, wash, was

Page 67
1. socks
2. block
3. jog
4. sorry
5. what
6. forgot
7. o'clock
8. was
9. October
10. body
11. bottom
12. shop
13. problem
14. wash
15. bottle
16. clock
17. Answers will vary; a sample answer is *washing*.

Pages 68–69
1. problem
2. October
3. was
4. clock
5. jog
6. block

7. shop
8. bottle
9. bottom
10. o'clock
11. forgot
12. body
13. what
14. sorry
15. socks
16. wash
17–20. Definitions and sentences will vary.

Page 70
1. whole, hope, joke, wrote, alone, hole, close
2. slow, blow, show, yellow, snow, know
3. goes, toe
4. November

Page 71
1. wrote
2. goes
3. hope
4. whole
5. know
6. alone
7. yellow
8. close
9. November
10. toe
11. snow
12. blow
13. hole
14. slow
15. show
16. joke
17. Answers will vary; a sample answer is *knowing*.

Pages 72–73
1. wrote
2. alone
3. joke
4. whole
5. close
6. November
7. toe
8. Snow
9. goes
10. show
11. hole
12. know
13. blow
14. hope
15. slow
16. yellow
17. dome
18. rodent
19. adobe
20. console
Sentences will vary.

Page 74
1. most, ago, hold, hello, open, over, comb, almost, both, gold
2. coat, loaf, toast, boat, road
3. cocoa

Page 75
1. comb
2. gold
3. ago
4. both
5. hello
6. hold
7. most
8. almost
9. open
10. over
11. loaf
12. coat
13. toast
14. road
15. boat
16. cocoa
17. Answers will vary; a sample answer is *toasts*.

Pages 76–77
1. ago
2. loaf
3. boat
4. almost
5. Both
6. most
7. road
8. Hello
9. over
10. comb
11. cocoa/toast
12. toast/cocoa
13. coat
14. hold
15. open
16. gold
17. no
18. yes
19. no
20. yes
Sentences will vary.

Page 78
1. book, took, cook, stood, wood, poor, foot, shook, cookies
2. sure, put, full, pull
3. should, would, could

Page 79
1. pull
2. stood
3. sure
4. poor
5. full
6. took
7. foot
8. should
9. wood
10. cookies
11. could
12. cook
13. put
14. would
15. shook
16. book
17. Answers will vary; a sample answer is *cooks*.

Pages 80–81
1. wood

2. cookies
3. foot
4. should
5. pull
6. put
7. stood
8. shook
9. poor
10. cook
11. sure
12. full
13. book
14. took
15. could
16. would
17–20. Definitions and sentences will vary.

Page 82
1. sneezed, smiling, hoped, shining, pleased, liked, taking, driving, closed
2. beginning, dropping, stopped, dropped, jogged, hopping, shopping

Page 83
1. jogged
2. beginning
3. closed
4. hoped
5. liked
6. shining
7. stopped
8. smiling
9. hopping
10. sneezed
11. taking
12. dropped
13. driving
14. pleased
15. dropping
16. shopping
17. Answers will vary; a sample answer is *pleasant*.

Pages 84–85
1. liked
2. hoped
3. beginning
4. dropping
5. dropped
6. taking
7. closed
8. hopping
9. stopped
10. pleased
11. sneezed
12. jogged
13. driving
14. shopping
15. shining
16. smiling
17–20. Definitions and sentences will vary.

Page 86
1. noon, tooth, school, too

Answer Key
Core Skills Spelling 3, SV 9781419034077

2. blue, Tuesday, true, few, knew, news

3. huge, used, June

4. who, two, move

Page 87
1. noon
2. news
3. who
4. tooth
5. move
6. school
7. blue
8. June
9. few
10. two
11. too
12. huge
13. true
14. used
15. knew
16. Tuesday
17. Answers will vary; a sample answer is *removed*.

Pages 88–89
1. Tuesday
2. too
3. knew
4. June
5. school
6. tooth
7. used
8. noon
9. blue
10. who
11. two
12. move
13. few
14. huge
15. news
16. true
17. casual
18. dispute
19. shrewd
20. pursue
Sentences will vary.

Page 90
1. curl, turn, Thursday, fur
2. girl, bird, first, dirt, third
3. world, word, work, worm
4. learn, earth
5. were

Page 91
1. worm
2. girl
3. Earth
4. first
5. third
6. turn
7. Thursday
8. word
9. dirt
10. were
11. learn
12. work
13. curl
14. world

15. fur
16. bird
17. Answers will vary; a sample answer is *worked*.

Pages 92–93
1. Thursday
2. learn
3. girl
4. work
5. earth
6. bird
7. were
8. fur
9. third
10. dirt
11. first
12. worm
13. curl
14. world
15. word
16. turn
17. yes
18. no
19. no
20. yes
Sentences will vary.

Page 94
1. dark, yard, art, market, garden, hard, father, March, arm, barn, start, star, card, sharp, bark
2. heart

Page 95
1. garden
2. market
3. March
4. card
5. barn
6. yard
7. dark
8. hard
9. father
10. sharp
11. start
12. art
13. star, star
14. heart, heart
15. bark, bark
16. arm
17. Answers will vary; a sample answer is *started*.

Pages 96–97
1. father
2. yard
3. bark
4. hard
5. barn
6. garden
7. market
8. heart
9. dark
10. star
11. March
12. sharp
13. start
14. card
15. arm
16. art

17–20. Definitions and answers will vary.

Page 98
1. coin, choice, spoil, boil, voice, soil, noise, pint, broil, join, oil
2. boy, royal, toy, joy, enjoy

Page 99
1. royal
2. oil
3. toy
4. joy
5. voice
6. spoil
7. join
8. coin
9. boy
10. enjoy
11. choice
12. noise
13. soil
14. broil
15. point
16. boil
17. Answers will vary; a sample answer is *joyfully*.

Pages 100–101
1. joy
2. voice
3. point
4. enjoy
5. choice
6. noise
7. boil
8. oil
9. broil
10. royal
11. coin
12. toy
13. spoil
14. soil
15. boy
16. join
17. yes
18. yes
19. no
20. no
Sentences will vary.

Page 102
1. isn't, weren't, doesn't, hadn't, mustn't, wouldn't, won't, shouldn't, aren't, wasn't, don't, couldn't, didn't, hasn't, haven't
2. can't

Page 103
1. won't
2. don't
3. couldn't
4. wouldn't
5. doesn't
6. wasn't
7. hadn't
8. mustn't
9. didn't
10. can't

11. hasn't
12. haven't
13. aren't
14. weren't
15. isn't
16. shouldn't
17. Answers will vary; a sample answer is *hadn't*.

Pages 104–105
1. wasn't
2. hadn't
3. wouldn't
4. aren't
5. couldn't
6. weren't
7. haven't
8. doesn't
9. didn't
10. can't
11. mustn't
12. don't
13. won't
14. hasn't
15. shouldn't
16. isn't
17. yes
18. yes
19. no
20. no
Sentences will vary.

Page 106
1. frog, along, long, off, belong, strong
2. walk, water, always, mall, tall, talk
3. bought, brought
4. because
5. draw

Page 107
1. strong
2. off
3. always
4. tall
5. long
6. talk
7. water
8. mall
9. brought
10. draw
11. frog
12. belong
13. along
14. walk
15. bought
16. because
17. Answers will vary; a sample answer is *talked*.

Pages 108–109
1. draw
2. frog
3. brought
4. strong
5. talk
6. long
7. tall
8. mall
9. always
10. along

11. bought
12. walk
13. off
14. water
15. belong
16. because
17. no
18. yes
19. no
20. yes
Sentences will vary.

Page 110
1. August, autumn
2. morning, popcorn, before, corner, storm, north, born, fork, sport
3. door, floor, four, pour
4. quart

Page 111
1. popcorn
2. fork
3. storm
4. corner
5. pour
6. north
7. autumn
8. morning
9. before
10. quart
11. floor
12. door
13. four
14. sport
15. born
16. August
17. Answers will vary; a sample answer is *northern*.

Pages 112–113
1. sport
2. before
3. floor
4. door
5. quart
6. four
7. popcorn
8. fork
9. autumn
10. August
11. pour
12. storm
13. north
14. morning
15. corner
16. born
17. wharf
18. corridor
19. ornament
20. coarse
Sentences will vary.

Page 114
1. house, sound, ground, found, about, hour, around, count, our
2. flower, town, tower, brown, power, down, owl

Page 115
1. house
2. sound
3. hour
4. tower
5. owl
6. down
7. power
8. about
9. flower
10. ground
11. found
12. count
13. brown
14. around
15. our
16. town
17. Answers will vary; a sample answer is *powerful*.

Pages 116–117
1. owl
2. brown
3. count
4. about
5. our
6. found
7. tower
8. town
9. ground
10. flower
11. down
12. sound
13. power
14. hour
15. house
16. around
17–20. Definitions and sentences will vary.

Page 118
1. near, hear, deer, ear, year, here, dear
2. care, where, stairs, chair, air, hair
3. fire, wire, tire

Page 119
1. hair
2. stairs
3. wire
4. dear
5. air
6. deer
7. hear
8. care
9. ear
10. year
11. near
12. where
13. tire
14. fire
15. here
16. chair
17. Answers will vary; a sample answer is *nearest*.

Pages 120–121
1. near
2. dear
3. here
4. year

5. fire
6. chair
7. hair
8. care
9. ear
10. hear
11. deer
12. air
13. wire
14. tire
15. Where
16. stairs
17. inspire
18. dairy
19. careless
20. dreary
Sentences will vary.

Page 122
1. taller, tallest, longer, longest, stronger, strongest, greater, greatest, sharper, sharpest
2. dirtier, dirtiest, funnier, funniest
3. hotter, hottest

Page 123
1. hotter
2. sharpest
3. sharper
4. strongest
5. dirtiest
6. taller
7. funniest
8. tallest
9. greater
10. longer
11. stronger
12. longest
13. hottest
14. greatest
15. funnier
16. dirtier
17. Answers will vary; a sample answer is *sharpening*.

Pages 124–125
1. hotter
2. hottest
3. sharper
4. sharpest
5. greater
6. greatest
7. stronger
8. strongest
9. taller
10. tallest
11. dirtier
12. dirtiest
13. longer
14. longest
15. funnier
16. funniest
17–20. Definitions and sentences will vary.